P9-EEO-736

THE

BORN-AGAIN CATHOLIC

Albert H. Boudreau

LIVING FLAME PRESS
LOCUST VALLEY, N.Y. 11560

Fourth printing 1983

Cover: Robert Manning

Copyright © 1980: Albert H. Boudreau

Nihil Obstat: Rev. Robert Hofstetter, *Censor Librorum* October 4,
1979

Imprimatur: Most Rev. James D. Niedergeses, Bishop of Nashville,
October 4, 1979

ISBN: 0-914544-26-8

All rights reserved. This book or parts thereof must not be
reproduced in any form without permission of the publisher.

Published by: Living Flame Press/Box 74/Locust Valley, N.Y.
11560

Printed in the United States of America

248.4
B661b

L.I.F.E. College Library
1100 Glendale Blvd.
Los Angeles, Calif. 90026

DEDICATION

To my wife, Sheila

031889

ACKNOWLEDGEMENT

I wish to express my thanks to my family for their constant support, to Sister Maria Edwards, Sister Margaret Turk and Father Philip Breen for their critical review of the manuscript, and to Bishop James Niedergeses for his support and encouragement.

SCRIPTURE REFERENCES

Scripture quotations, unless otherwise stated, were obtained from *The New American Bible,* with the permission of the Confraternity of Christian Doctrine.

Some quotations were taken from other versions:

Good News Bible (The Bible in Today's English Version), copyrighted 1976 by the American Bible Society (indicated by the reference TEV).

The Jerusalem Bible, Doubleday and Co., Garden City, N.Y., copyrighted by Darton, Longman and Todd, Ltd., and Doubleday and Co., Inc., 1966 (indicated by the reference JB).

The Holy Bible, King James Version, Thomas Nelson Inc., Camden, New Jersey, copyrighted by Thomas Nelson Inc., 1970 (indicated by the reference KJV).

The Living Bible, Tyndale House Publishers, Wheaton, Illinois, copyrighted 1971 by Tyndale House Publishers (indicated by the reference Living Bible).

CONTENTS

The Purpose of This Book

At every Sunday Mass I see men and women looking for something — yet apparently not finding it. They go through rites and rituals without ever discovering the reality behind them. Some seem to have been searching for so long that they're now convinced the "reality" can't be found; they keep attending Mass out of sheer habit.

But they're wrong. There *is* a reality to be found — the reality of God alive today — and he's reawakening men's hearts as never before. Certain movements in the Church are introducing spiritually hungry people to a "personal relationship" with God whom they know as "loving Father." Fear is gone, anxiety is gone, desperation and unbelief are gone; in their place are peace, joy and fulfillment which they never dreamed Christianity could offer. There are still millions of spiritually hungry Catholics not in contact with these movements who desperately need to hear this message of a "personal God" — a God who can add joy, peace and power to their lives. I have written this book for these people.

If we're going to investigate the "living reality" of God as "Father," I need to present a bit of authority. So I've used extensive references and made liberal use of quotes from sources whose authority is well established. These include Sacred Scripture, The Documents of Vatican II, writings of the Saints, and the thoughts of noted Christian writers. I have one further qualification. This personal relationship of which I write is a reality in my own life. I've come to know God as "Abba-Father" and I can testify to the powerful impact such a relationship has on one's life.

This was not always the case, however. My undergraduate theology studies taught me about God's existence but he remained an abstraction, a God of logic and reason, not a flesh and blood God. The God I studied never walked the shores of Lake Galilee healing sickness and casting out terror. He never said, "I am the way, the truth, and the life. Let me lead you to the Father. I can refresh you." The God I knew never hung bleeding from a cross. You can't love an abstraction nor be loved by it really. God is spirit — a spirit of love. You can't contain such love within the confines of a theology book. It transcends all bounds; it heals and sets free and the only way you can learn about such love is by experiencing it.

— My understanding of a "personal God" has not come easy. Eight years ago I was determined to leave the Church and give up Christianity; my search for reality had seemingly ended in failure. My Christian life at that point was dull, powerless and joyless. In desperation I sincerely prayed, "God, if you're real, show me." He did just that. I've now come to see that a personal relationship with God is not only possible for the average Christian, but it's the only way to fly. I've also come to see that this personal Christianity isn't new, it's not Protestant, and it's not a passing fad — the product of some movement. Instead, it's at the

8

heart of Christianity, at the center of Catholic teaching, and is indispensable for anyone who wants to live the Christian life with power, joy and satisfaction. A personal relationship with the Father is truly a "born-again" experience.

So what am I offering you in this book? First, some answers to those difficult questions — or should I call them doubts — about the "born-again" experience. Then I'll take you on a journey of discovery. You will see how the Church treated this experience in the past and discover the exciting new understanding she's developed today. Finally, I'll introduce you to a friend — I call him simply "Father" — and if you'll accept his invitation, he'll make your Christian life richer than you ever dared imagine.

The pages ahead illumine a promise made by the Father himself:

I will welcome you and be
a father to you
and you will be my sons
and daughters,
says the Lord Almighty.

2 Corinthians 6:18

CHAPTER 1

God Is Alive and Well

Two single-engine, private planes sped across a dark Indiana sky bound for Tennessee. Cessna 58 Delta trailed behind and to the left of Cardinal 385.

"Cardinal 385, this is 58 Delta."

"Go ahead George — err 58 Delta."

"Al, it looks like it's going to be clear sailing all the way home. The Lord sure has been good to us this weekend."

"Yeah, George, I think he's been watching over every single step. And now he's topped it off by giving us a tailwind. We'll make it home in less than four hours. Over."

"Great! Just keep that ole beacon of yours flashing and I'll follow you like a homesick hound. 58 Delta out."

"Roger. 385 out."

Two pilots winging their way through darkened skies. Two brothers in Christ experiencing his guiding hand. Two men of different religious backgrounds united in love and respect for one another.

I'll never forget that night as George and I flew wing on wing those 500 miles through star-filled skies. But as I reflect on it there was another experience we shared, even more unforgettable, which led up to that flight. It changed the two of us from powerless Christians to men sure of our faith, and best of all, enjoying it.

And that's what this book is all about: enjoying Christianity, and about the experience that makes it possible. As a Catholic active in today's Church, I encounter many views about this personage we call God; I see people acting out their Christianity in all sorts of ways. Granted, some seem disillusioned and almost spiritually dead, but at the other end of the spectrum are those whose Christian life is vital, strong and growing. These Catholics are talking about a change in their life which has made God alive. They are saying that Christianity now has power, joy and real satisfaction. Call it "personal Christianity," the "born-again" experience, or the "anointing of the Holy Spirit." Call it whatever you wish. The point is, this experience of a personal God is revolutionizing their lives, and by doing that, it is bringing life back to the Church.

But as a Church we have to take a hard look at this move toward personal Christianity. Is it really valid? Is it based on sound doctrine? And ultimately, is it from God? So this book also provides some evidence to help us judge personal Christianity. Now some people would not bother judging it; just let everyone do their own thing (as long as it's not obviously wrong). But that's a deadly attitude, and we as a Church can't afford it. We need to evaluate this personal Christianity, and by so doing, protect ourselves from the wolves of false doctrine.

One important way in which personal Christianity is entering today's Church is through renewal movements. While these movements may differ in their out

ward appearance, most share one underlying theme —
that of a God more personal, more intimate, more loving than you and I ever conceived him to be. But the
first reaction of most Catholics is: "Seems sort of Protestant to me." They eye every new movement with
suspicion. They hear people in the renewal saying
things that sound downright uncatholic, such as:

> . . . unless a man believes in Jesus Christ, true
> God and true man, and *accepts him as his own
> Savior,* the salvation that is offered to the
> whole of mankind will be of no avail to him.*

or:

> Whoever accepts Jesus, the incarnate Word of
> God, as his Lord and Savior, and is *born again*
> of the same Spirit by which Jesus himself was
> conceived . . . receives a share in his divine
> nature.
>
> Anne Field, O.S.B., *The Binding of the Strong Man,* pp. 85-86.

You might think such statements are evangelical
Protestantism or renewal movement rhetoric. Not so!
They're basic teachings of our Catholic faith: words
from St. Leo the Great, Pope of the Catholic Church
from 440 to 461 A.D.

If people in the renewal are saying these things, the
movement must be on to something. Apparently they've
discovered an essential Christian truth in this idea of a
personal relationship with God. Well then, you might
ask, what does the Church teach about this personal
relationship and why don't we hear more about the

---

*The emphasis here, and in quotations throughout the book, is the
author's.

subject?

To put it bluntly, our Church has a big problem. The Catholic Church, which for so many centuries taught us about Jesus' presence in the Eucharist, has trouble preaching clearly about our Father and Jesus who are asking us to become involved in an intimate personal relationship with them. The teaching is there in theory, but not in reality (except in some renewal movements). When the message is preached, it's painted in an intellectual, abstract language that doesn't reach the hearts of those who hear it.

Shortly after Vatican II closed its doors, an English theologian, Charles Davis, observed:

> Much speaking in different places on themes of renewal has brought me into contact with many people seeking to revivify their faith. I have found a sense of emptiness, but together with it a deep yearning for God. There is an emptiness at the core of people's lives, an emptiness waiting to be filled. They are troubled about their faith; they find it slipping. I am not speaking of those who are worried about recent changes. These people are not. But they are looking for something more; they are looking for something to fill the void in their lives, and what they hear does not do that. The more perceptive know they are looking for God. He seems to have withdrawn from the world and from them. They come to talks by speakers like myself. They hear about the new liturgy, about the new understanding of the layman's role, about collegiality, about the Church and the world, about a thousand and one new and exciting ideas. They are duly

impressed. *But who will speak to them quite simply of God as of a person he intimately knows, and make the reality and presence of God come alive for them once more?*

America, January 29, 1966.

Yes, that's it — we need to hear about a God who's alive and known personally. One of the architects of Vatican II, Leon Joseph Cardinal Suenens of Malines-Brussels, said essentially the same thing in an interview for *New Covenant* Magazine:

> As a pastor, I have been concerned for a long time with the need to make Christianity more personal for Christians who do not have much of a personal relationship to Christ. Many Christians do not experience this personal relationship as they should. Many are Christians out of custom, because their parents are, and so on. But at some point, *each person should be led to make a personal commitment to Christ.*

Interview, *New Covenant* Magazine, Vol. 2, No. 12,
Jn. 1973, pp. 2-3.

So you see, the basic problem today is that we Catholics are hearing Jesus' message dressed up in a technical, sacramental, theological language that's frankly too abstract. While there's a certain beauty in abstracting the Gospel, it fails to speak powerfully to God's people. Bishop Flores of San Antonio hit at the heart of this problem when he spoke of many Catholics who have been ''sacramentalized'' but never effectively ''evangelized.''* To be evangelized means, among

*Speech reported in the *Texas Catholic,* Nov. 1970.

14

other things, to hear the Gospel message and *understand* it. And one essential point of Jesus' Gospel — the one we're seeking now to understand — is our need for a personal relationship with God as Father through Jesus, or as some call it, the "born-again" experience.

In the pages ahead we're going to search for the truth of a personal relationship with God using plain English. In exploring this basic Christian truth which has been with the Church since it began, we'll see why certain historical events made it disappear for a while and why changing attitudes are now allowing it to be rediscovered. My message, therefore, is simple: the unbelievable thrill of experiencing God as Father is available today for everyone who wants it, and I intend to show you how it can happen in your own life.

A RELIGIOUS EXPERIENCE . . . OH, REALLY!

Just mention that you've had a religious experience and you'll see raised eyebrows all around, as if you'd been foisted by an evangelical rip-off. Most critics, however, won't even ask what you mean; they'll just lightly dismiss the whole matter as unworthy of their attention. When you do find one who'll talk, his argument will be something like: "This personal Christianity of yours, this born-again experience, gives me a hard time. It's too Protestant — you know, all wrapped up in emotionalism. It's just not for me."

Oh, I know the critics well. You see, I used to be one. But I was confused, and so are they. If they weren't confused, they'd never make such foolish statements. Yes, most things they say are without any foundation. Yet at this point I'm afraid — afraid that as we begin our search your views have already been colored by outspoken critics with shallow arguments. If you have any doubts about personal Christianity or this born-again experience, the remainder of this book should remove them. But for now let's look at where the critics are mistakenly pointing their finger and at least give you some doubts about your doubts.

You can talk about ''religious experience'' and mean many things, but if you'd ask me for my definition, I'd have to say, ''It's the experience of actually perceiving God's presence, not with my physical eyes, not with my mind alone, but with my spirit. In this experience I come to *know* God exists, and best of all, I know he calls me into himself. God is no longer a theology, a doctrine, a philosophy; but a living, personal reality. As I encounter his existence, every part of me — mind, will, emotions, and flesh — participates in that encounter.'' But these words wouldn't be enough. How can I tell you of the power of that contact? How can I describe its transforming warmth? What words could convey the beauty of his presence? What idea could capture the light of His Spirit? What way is there to express the inexpressible?

No, you can't scientifically dissect it. You can't put it in a theological box; religious experience is too big for that. This living encounter with the living God is Christianity as it was meant to be. God isn't some static concept — he's alive, and saints throughout the centuries have rediscovered this through the vitality of Christian experience. Yet there are those in our Church who are critical. They mistakenly label ''uncatholic'' anything they don't understand.

Take for instance this idea of being born again. To hear the critics talk it's a purely Protestant phenomenon. How easily they forget that Jesus himself introduced the term *(John 3:3),* and that the concept is actually basic to our Christianity. The problem lies with us Catholics who have buried that beautifully simple idea in a tangle of high sounding dogmas and rituals. Perhaps we'd be better off to do as our Protestant brothers do and simply use Jesus' born-again idea. After all, you can't beat his credentials and by using Jesus' teaching method Evangelicals boast the fastest growing arm of Christianity today; it's hard to argue with success like that.

So the basic idea of being born again is as Catholic as Sunday Mass. If it weren't, Pope John Paul II would never have said:

> This union of Christ with man is in itself a mystery. From the mystery is *born "the new man,"* called to become a partaker of God's life.
>
> *Redemptor Hominis, #18.*

The critic goes wrong because he didn't do his homework, while the Pope apparently did. You see whenever anyone starts to expound on the meaning of Christian experience he has a responsibility, the responsibility to check his arguments against competent theology. And there's plenty of it around — yes even on the topic of "religious experience" — yet few critics will take the time to dig for it.

Now it's the Church's duty to "test all things"; so that's just what happened when Catholics recently began to rediscover the richness of Christian experience. And not only did the Church check it out, but she gave it what theologians call *provisional theological justification* which is a way of saying, "This seems to be quite valid; go ahead while we study it further."

Why then do these critics continue to cut down the idea? Why are they closed to a born-again experience? The answer lies in that word *experience.* They're afraid of it. (I know I was.) Most Catholics, especially priests, seem to be conditioned to reject anything that smacks of religious experience. ''Emotionalism!'' they cry, and retreat to a *small* theological cage that keeps such things at bay. That's the way they've been brought up and it's quite a natural reaction, although unfortunate.

Now please understand me. I'm not saying that most priests are maliciously attacking personal Christianity; they are not. In fact, most are quite sincere in their objections, but their education has made them overly skeptical of all religious experience. Most priests who have been out of the seminary more than ten years have never studied the positive side of this issue, so they're simply not equipped to identify valid experiences. They studied only the evils of ''divisive enthusiasm'': Jansenism, Quietism, revivalism and the like — all distortions of true Christian experience. After ordination, their cautious attitude was probably reinforced by a few people they met. Surely anyone who's been in the ministry for a while has run across people with overactive imaginations, claiming supernatural insights and questionable experiences. So the critic's view remains negative.

''Ah-hah, you forgot one important thing,'' the critic will retort, ''When studying theology we learned that Christianity is based on *faith,* not on *experiences* which tend to come and go.'' And, of course, that's true but in teaching these things, the Church doesn't deny that religious experiences are valid. Quite the contrary, *faith* and *experience* are supposed to complement one another. The cautions are meant only to steer us clear of problems; not kill the idea, not rule out experience, not smother emotion. If you confine Christianity to faith alone, you confine it to the "sphere of the unobservable" — keeping it out of sight and making your religion merely an exercise of the mind.

But the critics protest, "Our studies show that these religious experiences are related to emotional, pietistic movements that keep cropping up and disappearing." True, movements do crop up and disappear with some regularity, but this argument really defeats itself. You see, personal Christianity — the born-again experience — actually cuts across all movements, denominations and man-made classifications. It does this because it's basic Christianity. The movements are simply rediscovering again and again a *basic* Christian truth. They haven't invented it — God did. Wherever genuine Christianity exists, you can be sure religious experience will also exist.

Catholic history abounds with stories of valid Christian experience. For instance, the *Spiritual Exercises* of St. Ignatius Loyola are used even today and have repeatedly been endorsed by popes and bishops. Yet every spiritual renewal in Christian history, whether valid or not, had critics who labeled it "fanaticism." (Someone once described a fanatic as "one who has stronger convictions than I have.")

Still the critics rave on, "It's all emotions! Emotion causes the experience. Emotion convinces someone they're saved. Emotion gives them the power to get rid of their bad habits — drinking, swearing and the like." I chuckle to myself recalling that I used to think that way. How wrong I was. "What's wrong with that argument?" you ask. Well, it first assumes that any Christian experience is tied to emotionalism.

19

In other words, a person gets so emotionally worked up that he imagines an experience with God. Now I'm not saying that such things never happen; they do, but to say that *all* Christian experience involves emotionalism is absurd.

What about the countless saints and holy people of the past 2000 years? Were they all emotionally unstable? The critic gets into this predicament because he observes a genuine Christian experience where the Holy Spirit touches a person's heart, and because it also contains an emotional reaction, he assumes the emotion causes the experience. After all, he can see the emotion while the Spirit remains invisible. And of course when people talk about what happened to them, what else can they describe: only the feelings, the sensations, the emotions. But emotion is the effect, not the cause.

Jesus himself told us to '' . . . love the Lord your God with all your heart, with all your soul, with all your mind, and with all your strength'' *(Mark 12:30).* In other words, with our whole selves and that includes our emotions. To dehumanize the spiritual life is to go against Jesus' teaching. He never intended that we roam a spiritual desert, isolated from feeling the Father's love. He never intended that we quench our emotions and act like religious robots. He wants us to act totally human as we encounter him.

In the second part of this argument, the critics claim that emotion *convinces* people they're saved. Now emotion by itself will not convince anyone of anything. People are convinced by truth. Yes, it's the truth of Jesus' Gospel believed through the power of the Holy Spirit. That's the convincing element in Christian experience. The same power of the Holy Spirit conquers those bad habits. Yet, like me, the critics won't be convinced until they themselves experience that interior revolution. It's only this marriage of truth and experience that can give you true assurance of the Father's love.

I used to have still another argument — one I thought quite good. "These emotional 'experiences' are caused by crisis in human affairs — wars, immorality, fears — which trigger psychological illusions or a form of self-hypnotism in certain unbalanced people." While this argument sounded authoritative, it was actually filled with error. First, there's no consistent connection between social-political crises and personal Christianity. You see, there has been no end to crises throughout history, and critics often can attach a genuine move of the Spirit to some parallel crisis in history. Yet there are instances where crises did not cause spiritual renewals, or where renewals occurred without corresponding crises. How do you explain these?

Now the second part of this argument is a bit more subtle. Perhaps a personal crisis, a strong desire, or a revival atmosphere can set off psychological forces which lead a person to imagine he has experienced a spiritual renewal. When you study actual situations, however, you find such variety in the types of experience and in the people who claim the experience that you're at a loss to find a unifying thread. And people seem to find this experience as often when they're alone as when they attend evangelical services and meetings.

Of course you could argue, "All right, it doesn't matter where or how you have the experience, but these people are still a bit unbalanced." Well, a group of psychologists thought the same some time ago and set out to test their theory. They chose two groups as much alike as possible, except that one group claimed to know Jesus as personal savior, experiencing the power of the Holy Spirit, while the other group, the control group, did not. Much to their surprise, the "Spirit-filled" Christians were better balanced psychologically than the control group. Their argument backfired, and so did mine. What they proved through science I found through experience: personal Christianity is based on a genuine religious experience and has nothing to do with psychological imbalances, self-hypnotism, or the like. In fact, it's the only real Christianity there is.

Psychologists can only look at Christian experience purely from a scientific standpoint. They can identify our basic psychological needs, such as "identity" and "purpose"; they can observe that personal Christianity supplies those needs; but they cannot judge whether any experience is genuine. That task falls to the Church, using theology and Scripture. The Church alone is equipped to judge the things of God.

Now there's one argument against personal Christianity that I've never shared with the other critics — I've always believed that Christians were somehow "special." Yet the critics will charge, "These turned-on Christians consider themselves a chosen elite, people who have a pipeline to God. Essentially, they are trying to manipulate God." Perhaps the critics suspect that we "something special people" have been listening to fanatical preachers, to evangelists like St. Peter who called Christians "a chosen race, a royal priesthood, a holy nation . . ."; or St. Paul who told us we were "fellow citizens of the saints and members of the household of God"; or Jesus who called us "the light of the world." Maybe we've been reading fanatical literature like *The Documents of Vatican II* where the Church Fathers speak of our "exalted status" as Christians (The Church, #14). Yes, the Catholic Church has always taught that Christians are special. Perhaps the critics should ask instead, "What's wrong with the 'ordinary' Christian who fails to recognize his specialness?"

Cardinal Suenens* points out that we are not called *Jesusites,* that is, mere followers of Jesus; but *Christians,* from the word *Christ,* meaning "the Anointed One." We Christians are anointed with the same Holy Spirit that Jesus possessed and in my book that's something special.

*A New Pentecost?, p. 166.

Yet we see "normal" Christians barely making it on the average, living in spiritual doldrums, while "abnormal" (born-again) Christians are happy to be Christians — yes, even excited about it. Now which is really normal? Could it be that the "normal" Christians are actually *subnormal?* Could it be that they've missed the whole point of Christianity? Could it be that they're settling for second best?

Now what about the criticism that these "elite" Christians think they have God at their beck and call? Is that any way for Christians to act? Yes, it certainly is. You'll find Jesus and the Apostles constantly telling Christians to pray believing that their prayers have been answered. So the whole issue boils down to a point of philosophy. The turned-on Christians believe in taking Jesus at his word — no compromising, no watering down; while the critics think Jesus was overdoing it a bit. They say we shouldn't take his message too seriously. "The culture of those days was different . . . you've got to be practical."

How can we reduce Christianity to an intellectual

exercise: impotent, over-formalized, over-comfortable? How can we "make a pretense of religion but negate its power" *(2 Timothy 3:5)?* The Father never designed Christianity to be lived under human power. It simply won't work that way. The power is supposed to come from God himself and it's not meant to come in some abstract way, but in a way any Christian can actually feel. You see, we are talking about real power, power beyond any intellectual truth that inspires us; beyond a set of moral laws to govern our behavior; beyond simply feeling good about ourselves and the world. St. Paul speaks of:

> . . . the *immeasurable scope of his power* in us who believe. It is like the strength he showed in raising Christ from the dead and seating him at his right hand in heaven.
>
> *Ephesians 1:19-20*

So the real issue is: "Do we believe in his power?"

Lastly, the critics will bring up the idea of intense, enthusiastic, religious experiences not producing strong commitments. They claim, "Turned-on Christians simply don't last long; when troubles come, Jesus goes." Well, I can best answer that criticism with my own experience and that of millions like me. We've all experienced the joy of personal Christianity, yet we've also been visited by those "dark nights of the soul" — still our commitment stands. Why? Because the critics fail to see that our experience resulted from a commitment; emotions flowed because we first made a decision; our "turned-on" status endured because we met — not a philosophy or doctrine — but a person, Jesus Christ.

Granted, sometimes born-again Christians fall

away, but that's also true of ordinary Christians. From what I've observed, the "turned-on" variety endure far better than the average. And if some born-again sheep have gone astray, could it be perhaps that there was no shepherd willing to understand and guide?

So all the arguments against personal Christianity, when you really study them, are empty excuses — excuses which allow the critic to escape the reality of religious experience. By dismissing personal Christianity, the critic labels of no account Catholics such as Leon Joseph Cardinal Suenens and Protestant leaders such as Dr. Billy Graham. He throws out as worthless the work of dedicated Catholic theologians who put their stamp of approval on this experience, not to mention thousands of priests and nuns who daily live the richness of personal Christianity.

And today born-again Christian ranks include doctors, lawyers, scientists, psychologists, military leaders, business executives, politicians, and yes, even presidents. You can question the credibility of one or two witnesses, but when born-again Christians number in the millions, you can't dismiss them lightly.

Perhaps we've lost sight of our ultimate destiny: isn't it union with the Father? And if Jesus told us to enter *now* the Kingdom, don't we *now* begin (though imperfectly) that very same union? And can true union with the Father be lifeless — without experience, without emotion, without feeling? I think not. I know not. So my premise is this: any Catholic can (and should) have this born-again experience. Any Catholic can truly know he's called to a living relationship with a living, personal God.

Now most theologians would say, "When we speak of a 'personal God' we mean that God *has personality;* he's not just an abstract force." Fine, but our investigation will not stop at speaking of a God who *has* personality; no, we're going beyond that to speak of a God who is interested in having a *personal relationship* with the creatures he has made, namely, you and me. So let's define exactly what we're talking about at the outset. Don't worry that you find it hard to agree with. Perhaps you may even disagree with it completely. In the pages to follow I hope to make this definition come alive for you. Simply listen to it for now and understand what it's saying — that's all I ask.

DEFINITION: A *Personal God* not only *has* personality as described by the Scriptures, but also is *personally involved* with mankind. He reveals himself as a loving, concerned Father who reaches out to touch his children's lives in everyday circumstances. His concern extends to the most minute detail of those lives as he seeks to have us know him through a deep and intimate *relationship.* This relationship comes from sharing his divine life.

In speaking so much about relationships, you might feel that I'm overdoing it. Not so. In fact some people have gone so far as to say, "Christianity isn't a religion, it's a relationship." Now I wouldn't deny that Christianity is a religion, but I must agree with their basic idea. They're saying that the heart of Christianity doesn't lie in religious rules, or doctrines, or theology, or pious sayings of holy men; but goes beyond that to put Christians into an intimate relationship with God himself. A relationship which makes them, in a concrete way, sons and daughters of God.

The prophet Ezekiel had a vision 2500 years ago: he saw Israel's spiritual life as a valley of dry bones. Today some people would prefer Ezekiel style, dry-bone Christians to a valley where the bones are alive. Yes, moving bones are scary things, but in them there is life and hope.

SOURCES FOR THE SEARCH

If we're going to explore the meaning of a basic Christian truth, we would do it better with authority. The authority we should seek is much more than human authority — it should be founded upon God himself. So let's stop at this point and examine the sources quoted in these pages.

Scripture

When the Sadducees came to Jesus to try out their ideas on him, he rebuked them:

> You are badly misled because you fail to understand the Scriptures and the power of God.
>
> *Matthew 22:29*

To avoid being misled, we must know what the Scriptures say about our relationship to God. All doctrines, no matter how profound, must be based upon (and agree with) principles laid down in Scripture. St. Paul, writing to Timothy, said:

> All Scripture is inspired of God and is useful for teaching — for reproof, correction, and training in holiness.
>
> *2 Timothy 3:16*

Now Scripture is the revelation to man *in written form* of God himself. Just as Jesus (the Word made flesh) is the foundation stone of his Church, so Scripture (the written Word) must be the foundation of all theology and doctrines.

But there can be a problem here. Scripture must be believed for it to have authority, and some modern schools of thought downplay the inspiration of Scripture to the point of making it useless. We need only to study the New Testament to see what a love Jesus had for Scripture; he quoted it constantly. Can we have any less love for his Word and still be considered his followers? At Vatican II the Church Fathers spelled out the official Catholic view of Scripture:

> Therefore, since everything asserted by the inspired authors or sacred writers must be held to be asserted by the Holy Spirit, it follows that the books of Scripture must be acknowledged as teaching *firmly, faithfully,* and *without error* that truth which God wanted put into the sacred writings for the sake of our salvation.
>
> *Documents of Vatican II,* Dogmatic Constitution on Divine Revelation, #11.

Need we say more?

Vatican II Documents

The Second Vatican Council (1962-1965) was an historic event for any Catholic living at the time. The actions of that Council have touched us all, and whether we like them or not, the changes have been far-reaching. Like the twenty ecumenical councils preceding it, Vatican II proclaimed the teachings and beliefs of the Church. It was challenged, however, with the task of explaining the Church and Christian faith to a modern, educated world. This wasn't a simple case of theologians talking to other theologians about deep spiritual matters. No, this council was speaking to the world, to the laity, to you and me about some very practical matters. So if we're to study this personal relationship with God as Father, we had better look to the Church Fathers at Vatican II.

Basic Teachings Document

In 1973 the National Conference of Catholic Bishops published a document called *Basic Teachings for Catholic Religious Education.* This landmark booklet boiled down the great weight of Catholic doctrine and teaching into twenty-eight pages. It presents the essentials of Catholic Christianity to instructors in various religious education programs. If the conclusions we draw in this investigation are valid, we should expect the ''Basic Teachings'' document to agree with them. The introduction to the booklet states:

> It is necessary that these basic teachings be central in all Catholic religious instruction, be never overlooked or minimized, and be given adequate and frequent emphasis.

Cardinal Suenens

Leon Joseph Cardinal Suenens, Archbishop of Brussels-Malines, Belgium, was a leader of Vatican II. His book *A New Pentecost?* is a contemporary view of Christian Renewal Movements. Pope Paul VI remarked, ''I wish to make allusion to the book written by Cardinal Suenens entitled *A New Pentecost?* in which he describes and justifies this expectation of renewal.'' In voicing his approval of this book, the late Pope has given us a valuable asset in our investigation since the book expresses the up-to-date views of a leading figure in today's Church.

St. Leo the Great

Lest anyone say that I'm presenting only the latest ''renewal'' ideas, I've included numerous quotes from St. Leo the Great, elected Pope in 440 A.D. He was noted for his strong proclamation of basic Christian truths in a time when heresies plagued the Church. A modern translation of his sermons, *The Binding of the Strong Man* by Anne Field O.S.B., will be our source for St. Leo's teachings.

Other Christian Writers

Although the five sources just listed will be the primary tools in this investigation, I'll quote other Christian writers to gain more insight and to demonstrate that this concept of a personal relationship is not an isolated one.

UNDERSTANDING THE "WHAT"

The ideas expressed in this chapter were not meant to convince you of anything; that will be my job in the pages ahead. Right now I ask you simply to understand ''what'' it is I'm talking about — a personal, loving, intimate, relationship with God as Father. I hope that you are also beginning to understand what effects this kind of relationship can have on a person's life.

C.S. Lewis, in *Mere Christianity,* wrote:

If you want joy, power, peace, eternal life, you must get close to, or even into, the thing that has them. They are not a sort of prize which God could, if He chose, just hand out to anyone. They are a great fountain of energy and beauty spurting up at the very center of reality. If you are close to it, the spray will wet you: if you are not, you will remain dry. Once a man is united to God, how could he not live forever? Once a man is separated from God, what can he do but wither and die?

Mere Christianity, p. 153.

We are off now, in search of that fountain. We seek to draw close to it and find joy, power, peace and eternal life.

CHAPTER 2

Tradition Battles Change

Recently a TV news program told about a man fighting changes demanded by his local government. He barricaded himself in his house, took out his trusty shotgun, and proceeded to blast his disapproval at the police. Eventually he was captured and carted off to jail.

Now we Catholics are rooted in a centuries-old tradition which makes our resistance to change almost as strong. But this resistance to new ideas isn't necessarily bad. In fact, sometimes it's quite a healthy instinct — a safety valve preventing us from going off on all sorts of religious tangents. However, when we carry our resistance to the extreme, when we take the shotgun and barricade approach, we can easily kill any genuine movement of God in our lives. You see, God never imposes his will on us; he never forces us to change. Our free will is never violated. So we, on our own, have to strike a balance and judge with open minds.

I'm asking you, for the moment, to put down your shotgun and step out from behind the barricade. I'm asking you, as a mature individual, to look with an open mind at this thing I'm calling ''personal Christianity.'' I'm asking you to judge it on the basis of the facts presented in these pages.

Of course you have the right, even the duty, to ask, "Why wasn't personal Christianity part of the Catholic tradition I was brought up in? Maybe it's a passing fad, hatched by some renewal movement." You have the right to put it on trial. But I must warn you, I have my witnesses ready in the pages ahead: the Church Fathers, noted Christian writers, the Saints and of course my star witness — Jesus.

In this chapter we'll start by looking at this mysterious thing called "tradition": a really fascinating subject. To a large degree it's the one thing that sets us apart as Catholic Christians. Traditions also determine which things can change in our Church and which cannot; so this brief look will give us a few ground rules for judging change. Next we'll explore some events in our Catholic history which tended to distort our views of personal Christianity; and finally we'll turn to the Church Fathers and let them steer us back on the right track.

TRADITIONS

In our two thousand year history the Church has changed remarkably. If through some sort of time machine we could be transported to another era in Church history, chances are we'd be quite uncomfortable with the way the Church looked and acted. The Mass would be different. Prayer would be different. Even people's ideas about what the Church *is* would be different. We probably wouldn't like it. You see, throughout Church history changes have been taking place gradually, and a person could live a long life without seeing much change. Yet changes have been occurring, and quite consistently. So much so that

Vatican II called the Church "a pilgrim people" who move continually toward their goal — God himself.

It's hard for us to believe sometimes that the Mass we attend nowadays — so changed from only two decades ago — is actually patterned after the Mass of the early Church. What seems new is, in fact, quite old. That "traditional Latin Mass," prior to Vatican II, would have been new and revolutionary to Christians of the early Church. Well, what's the message here? Simply this: the Church and her traditions are now, and always have been, in a state of change; sometimes rapid, sometimes slow, but always changing. Structures, liturgies, traditions and many external trappings have evolved from one age to another. But wait a minute. Weren't we taught that the traditions of the Church are sacred and don't change?

A very good question indeed. We begin to find the answer by first understanding that much of what we call "tradition" in our Church is actually linked to the culture of the times. In other words, it's connected to that place where we, the Church, happen to be in our history. Vatican II pointed this out:

> Living in various circumstances during the course of time, the Church, too, has used in her preaching the discoveries of different *cultures* to spread and explain the message of Christ to all nations.
>
> *Documents of Vatican II,* The Church Today, #58.

Recently Cardinal Suenens brought up this same point when he observed:

> Let us recognize honestly that the institutional Church, as we have defined it, is largely in-

debted to its *environment,* as every one of us is. This can explain, without always justifying, that "weight of history" which encumbers its movement and accumulates extraneous elements which, like sediment, tarnish the true image of the Church.

A New Pentecost?, p. 16

Yes, that worldly environment can enter the Church's life and "tarnish the true image." Sometimes even the basic message of Jesus is lost or confused. So most of the Church's great councils, like Vatican II, were called to set in order what had gotten out of order. This disorder usually sprang from outdated traditions which put tarnish on the true image. Vatican II declared:

It (Vatican Council II) proposes again the decrees of the Second Council of Nicaea, the Council of Florence, and the Council of Trent. And at the same time, as part of its own pastoral solicitude, this Synod urges all concerned to work hard to prevent or *correct any abuses, excesses, or defects* which may have crept in here and there, and to restore all things to a more ample praise of Christ and of God.

Documents of Vatican II, The Church, #51.

Well then, what can we say at this point about traditions? We can say that they often enter the Church from the outside world, that they're often rooted in the culture of the times, that they sometimes distort the message of Jesus Christ, and that they *can* (and often must) be altered by the Church. It's at this point that we can make a clear definition of tradition.

SPELLING TRADITION

If you're like me, you sometimes got frustrated by the changes of Vatican II. But this could have been avoided, I believe, if we as a Catholic people understood one basic principle: *Tradition* in our Church must be spelled two different ways. No, we aren't talking about a religious spelling lesson. It's simply a tool some theologians are using today to explain a principle of Catholic Christianity which has existed from the Church's beginning.

What we need to do now is name two categories or divisions of tradition. For the first we'll use a capital "T" so as to spell it Tradition. In the other division we'll use a small "t" and spell it tradition. When you see the underlined "t" or "T" you'll know we're talking about these two definitions.

Now Tradition means those parts of our Catholic heritage which are considered *unchangeable* realities — points of truth given to us by divine inspiration. One such Tradition is respect for the Bishop of Rome (the Pope) as the Church's earthly head. Another is Jesus' presence in the Eucharist. Also included is the teaching authority of the Church. The basic form of the Mass would be another.

It's in this sense of the word Tradition that the Church Fathers wrote:

Hence there exists a close connection and communication between sacred Tradition and sacred Scripture. For both of them, flowing from the same divine wellspring, in a certain way merge into a unity and tend toward the same end. For sacred Scripture is the word of God inasmuch as it is consigned to writing under the inspiration of the divine Spirit. To the successors of the apostles, sacred Tradition hands on in its full purity God's word, which was entrusted to the apostles by Christ the Lord and the Holy Spirit.

Documents of Vatican II, Dogmatic Constitution on Divine Revelation, #9.

So the Church looks both to Tradition and sacred Scripture for the principles she'll follow. The two sources don't compete with one another, but rather work together in harmony, guiding the Church as she faces new decisions. They enrich our belief in Christianity, adding wholesomeness to it. With this point in mind, the Apostle Paul wrote:

Therefore, brothers, stand firm. Hold fast to the Traditions you received from us, either by our word or by letter.

2 Thessalonians 2:15

Without Traditions our Church would not have the richness and beauty we've known and loved.

Well now, what are the traditions of our second category? They're things taken from the cultures of various times and places which also enrich our Church, yet are *changeable.* Vatican II observed:

. . . she (the Church) can enter into communion with various cultural modes, to her own enrichment and theirs too.

Documents of Vatican II, The Church Today, #58.

Examples of traditional culture are:
a. The language of the Mass

b. Sunday as the Lord's Day

c. Priestly vestments

d. The position of the altar

e. Deacons, lay ministers of the Eucharist, and lectors

f. Types of music for religious services

g. The form of the rituals used when administering sacraments

h. Nun's habits — or the lack thereof

i. The emphasis on reading scripture

j. Methods of teaching religion

These are just a few examples — the list is virtually endless. However, it should become clear to you now that Vatican II, like most other Councils, acted to change traditions, not Traditions. In fact most of the twenty-one Great Ecumenical Councils reaffirmed the Traditions of the Church. We became uneasy when we thought Vatican II was changing the unchangeable Traditions but, in fact, it was not.

Let's take a moment to look at those things which make traditions change. I would classify them into three categories:

1. The Church as a Pilgrim People

Vatican II called us, the Church, a Pilgrim People:

> The Church, "like a pilgrim in a foreign land, *presses forward* amid the persecutions of the world and the consolations of God."

Documents of Vatican II, The Church, #8,
quoting St. Augustine's "Civ. Dei."

The Council said something really profound here. It expressed the truth that we as a whole Church are moving toward something and that something is union with God himself. But by calling us pilgrims, it said that we're not yet there — our goal still lies ahead. In practical terms this means we should always expect to see the Church changing; always expect the Church to find better ways of perfecting herself. Vatican II said that . . .

> . . . the Church, embracing sinners in her bosom, is at the same time holy and always *in need of being purified,* and incessantly pursues the path of penance and renewal.
>
> *Documents of Vatican II,* The Church, #8.

St. Leo the Great also talked about this idea of growth in holiness. Over fifteen hundred years ago he said:

> . . . this life still has to grow; it cannot be stationary. Anyone who is not moving forward is bound to slip back. If we are not gaining ground, we are losing it.
>
> Anne Field, O.S.B., *The Binding of the Strong Man,* p. 98.

The Fathers of the Church said in effect: ''Expect the Church to be changing as it grows in holiness. Expect traditions to change or be altered if that's what it takes. Expect us to reject static attitudes and press toward our goal: God himself.'' So we conclude that traditions must change simply because we are a Church dedicated to change whenever it's necessary. We must keep moving towards perfection.

2. The Ecumenical Councils

Each of the twenty-one Ecumenical Councils brought change to the Church. In our lifetime it seems that only Vatican II made significant changes, but that's because we normally don't think in historical terms. We fail to see that the Nicene Creed was the "latest thing" introduced to the Church in 325 A.D. as a result of the Council of Nicaea. New regulations also followed the Council of Chalcedon in 451 A.D. Now monks would have to be in submission to their Bishops, the clergy could no longer be in business or engage in farming, and ordination was not permitted without a pastoral charge. The list is long indeed. Each Council continued the Church's pilgrim journey by way of new or modified doctrines and laws.

3. Cultural Influences of Society

At first glance you might think this third category would have had the least effect on changing traditions. Not so. In fact it has played a major role in shaping the Church throughout its two thousand year history. But why is this so if the Church's origin is God and he's changeless? The answer is simple. The Church is made up of men and women, human beings who carry with them the culture in which they live. Our culture is so much a part of us that we scarcely know we're projecting it into everything we do — and that includes our life within the Church. If the Church was made up only of God, this wouldn't be so but as long as the Church is composed of human beings, our culture cannot help but be thrust into its very heart. Sometimes this is good; often it is not. So the Church must continually judge the culture of the times.

In concluding our discussions on change, I would like to leave you with two thoughts. The first has to do with the very nature of the Church. When I was growing up, prior to Vatican II, the popular attitude was that the Church "represented" God here on earth. Because it was the official go-between, it was holy, infallible and unchanging. The idea seemed to be put forward that God never changed so the Church never changed. It was this idea that made Vatican II so hard to digest. In this discussion we've learned that we should really look at the Church as the "people of God" on the move. As individuals change and grow in holiness, the Church as a collection of those individuals also has to change and grow. The second thought then stems from the idea of a changing Church. Change, of and by itself, is not necessarily a good thing. Change simply for the sake of change is not a good thing. Change without true discernment of God's will is not a good thing. Change must be rooted in the authentic teachings of Jesus Christ and be guided by sacred Scripture and the true Traditions of our Church.

THE IMPERSONAL GOD CULTURE

Now we can get to the heart of this chapter. Our discussion on tradition and change laid the groundwork for a most important topic: how this foolish idea of an impersonal God crept into the Church's life. I say crept in because no one ever planned that it be there. However, it didn't just happen. Cultural, political and religious forces acted in very decisive ways to make it happen, and that's what we need to examine here. To do this we'll take a quick look at church history to see where and how events happened to shape this idea of an impersonal God. Of course Church history is much more complex than this outline suggests. We'll leave out many details, but the general conclusions are still quite valid.

First, let's look at the Church in the century prior to Vatican II. We'll do this through the eyes of Cardinal Suenens:

> When I was young, the Church was presented to us as a hierarchical society: it was described as ''juridically perfect,'' having within itself all the powers necessary to insure and promote its own existence. This view reflected an image of the Church which was closely modeled on civil, even military society: there was a descending hierarchy, a uniformity which was considered as an ideal, and a tight discipline which extended to the smallest detail, governing the life of both cleric and lay person and imposing even upon bishops a whole series of bureaucratic servitudes.

A New Pentecost?, pp. 1-2.

Now this doesn't sound like the ''early Church'' — the Church of the Apostles. That Church, while certainly lacking the refinements of theology and scripture we enjoy today, nevertheless is widely admired because of its depth of faith and commitment. When I say ''depth of faith and commitment,'' I mean even to death itself. Reading the Acts of the Apostles you get a picture of a Church quite different from the one Cardinal Suenens just described. There was less emphasis on structure and hierarchy, and more on an active faith in the risen Jesus alive in the hearts of his people. He was a personal Savior to them and the Father, a very personal God. Despite tremendous persecution, that early Church grew rapidly and produced such a strong witness that eventually the whole Roman Empire became Christian. If we're going to understand what happened to change that early Church, we need to focus on one critical event: the Roman Empire accepting Christianity. We can feel the effects of that decision even today. Cardinal Suenens again gives us insight by reflecting on the transition which took place in the early Church:

> Between the third and sixth centuries, however, there was an *historic process of evolution.* This exaggerated the juridical and institutional aspects of the Church, as well as the distinction between clergy and laity, which finally resulted in there being two classes of persons within the Church.
>
> *A New Pentecost?*, pp. 139-140.

The trigger for this "historic process of evolution" was the Emperor Constantine's conversion to Christianity around 313 A.D. All at once Christianity was the "in thing" for citizens of the Empire. Becoming Christian was the prudent thing to do; after all, the Emperor was Christian, and anyone with a lick of sense would try to be in step with him. The business man, for instance, knew that to succeed you had to conform to the government, so he "joined" the Church. Whatever their reasons, many people followed suit.

To some, this great influx of "new Christians" must have seemed like quite a victory. The whole world was coming to Jesus Christ — but was it? The "new Christians" weren't really interested in *conversion* as much as *conformity.*

So in one fell swoop a highly-structured society was impressed upon the Church and seemingly overwhelmed it. Some say that Constantine, a newly converted Christian, actually presided over the Council of Nicaea, the first of the great Ecumenical Councils. Religion and politics were even more closely intertwined now. The marriage between the secular world and the Church was highlighted by an event which many Church historians look upon as tragic. On February 27, 380 A.D. Theodosius, a Roman emperor of the East, proclaimed a new religious policy:

> We desire that all peoples who fall beneath the sway of our imperial clemency should profess the faith which we believe to have been communicated by the Apostle Peter to the Romans and maintained in its traditional form to the present day . . . And we *require* that those who follow this rule of faith should embrace the name of Catholic Christians, adjudging all others madmen and ordering them to be designated as heretics.
>
> Quoted in *A Short History of Christianity,*
> by Martin E. Marty, p. 99.

Consequently, it wasn't the things in a man's heart that brought him to Jesus, it was the Emperor's law. Jesus came to proclaim, among other things, freedom from the Jewish Law and religious legalism. Now the Church which bore his name was plunged into a worse legalism, a civil-religious legalism. You joined the Church or you were an outcast. There was no middle ground, no call to search your heart.

With society and the Church "married" so to speak, the Church adopted the forms of hierarchy common to society at that time. Today we have difficulty appreciating the kind of highly-structured culture in which the Church suddenly found itself. Lacking today's educational system a man was destined to grow up, marry, raise a family and die in the same social class. He was essentially locked into place on the social ladder, seldom moving more than one rung up or down throughout his whole life if, indeed, he moved at all. As the Church evolved into a structured society, the members of the Church hierarchy became more and more rigid in their positions. They were the educated — the laity, the uneducated. The Church hierarchy did the leading — the laity, the following. It was a kind of religious caste system.

Now you should realize that this was a very practical way to proceed and nobody really thought of it as being odd (or overstructured). It was actually very much in keeping with the common man's view of society. He saw the King as head of a social and legal order, with the court officials below the King, district rulers below them, etc., until the chain of authority ended with his local village official. When the Church took over that form of society, the common man saw much the same thing in the Church and it didn't surprise him one bit. It seemed very logical. God (who the Scriptures describe as a King) was over the bishops, who in turn were over the priests, who were over the laity. Now the local official had the authority of the King to back him up, so logically the priest had (through the hierarchy) the authority of God to back him up. It all made sense and fit quite comfortably into the common man's concept of how things ought to be. In his eyes the Church was not the assembly of God's people, but the official representative of God.

Imagine if you will a common man going up to the King's guard, "Ex — excuse me, Sir. I'd like to see the King. We have a few problems in the village and I

45

need to discuss them with the King.''

''Talk with the King? . . . You? Get out of here before I have you thrown in the dungeon.'' And with a shove the guard would send him on his way.

Yes, the common man knew better than to try that approach. His best bet, and by far the safest, was to see his local village official. And if that same man wanted advice on spiritual matters, he would see the priest, his ''local official'' in the Kingdom of God; he would not bother the King of Heaven. So it's easy to see how men began to relate to God in such an indirect manner. A personal relationship with God Almighty was as far from men's thinking as a personal relationship with the King himself.

As we shall see later, the Scriptures clearly teach that our heavenly Father wants us to relate to him personally, not through a chain of command. Throughout history there have been men and women able to see the difference between these two ideas. They had fellowship with the Father as it should be but they were relatively few. The basic tenor of Christian thought throughout these centuries was one of a God as distant from the ordinary man as the King or Emperor. In fact, a popular concept in those days was that a Christian King in effect established ''the Kingdom of God'' here on earth. This concept, of course, ignored the teaching of Jesus who said, ''the Kingdom of God is within you'' *(Luke 17:21 KJV)*.

THE ROAD BACK

Modern society has pretty much left rigid structuring behind and today men and women easily move up and down the social ladder. The Church, however, has retained much of this centuries-old structuring. It never taught a doctrine of an impersonal God, but it likewise (until recently) never corrected the traditions which preserved that idea. A chief outcome of Vatican II was a fresh look at this whole area of how God and man should relate to one another. Many outdated concepts, leftovers from the old structured society, were thrown out or modified; so the Council moved to

> . . . correct any abuses, excesses, or defects
> which may have crept in here and there.
>
> *Documents of Vatican II,* The Church, #51.

Vatican II made a frontal attack on the old concepts by re-emphasizing a doctrine called the ''Body of Christ.'' St. Paul introduced this concept to the early Church and Pope Pius XII re-introduced it in his ''Mystici Corporis Christi.'' They simply said that the Church should be pictured as a human body, and each Church member as an organ who serves that body in some essential way. If we do, in truth, see members who are higher or seemingly more important than others, we should think of them as an organ in the body who has more prominent duties to perform. For instance, the eye would seem more important than a finger, yet both perform an essential service for the body. The eye cannot be used as a finger, nor can the finger make a very good eye. Every organ in the body has different duties to perform, yet they are all essential to a normal healthy body. The Church Fathers were saying, ''There's a basic equality of all persons in the Church. Although each is called to fulfill a different function we form, as a Church, a single *People of God.''* The U.S. Bishops, in their ''Basic Teachings'' document, put it this way:

The Church is a community sharing together the life of Christ, a people assembled by God. Within this assembly there is a *basic equality of all persons.* There are different responsibilities in the Church. For example, the ministerial priesthood is essentially different from the ''priesthood of the people.'' But all are united and *equal* as the one People of God.

Basic Teachings for Catholic Religious Education, #21.

This ''basic equality'' concept is revolutionary compared to the hierarchical Church we discussed earlier, yet it's very much in agreement with the doctrines of the early Church. So today we find ourselves in transition. We're moving from the structural, hierarchical Church to one patterned after the purity of doctrine that was the early Church's lifeblood. We have much going for us in this move: theology, Scripture scholarship and Tradition to lead the way. Yet at the same time, we've been badly wounded by old ideas which distorted the message of Jesus. We still have to face up to this if we want true renewal in the Church. Cardinal Suenens has remarked:

I do not think that we can fail to be struck by the too frequent contrast between a Christian as outlined by Peter on the day following Pentecost and a Christian of today as the second millennium of the Christian era draws to a close. We have to open our eyes to this state of affairs if we hope to see the renewal of the Church become a reality: the Church is what its members are, no more, no less.

A New Pentecost?, p. 122.

This isn't merely the opinion of one Church Father; it's a concept at the very heart of Christianity today. Pope Paul VI in a general audience spoke of this future Church saying:

> We shall have, therefore, a period of greater freedom in the life of the Church and of her individual members. It will be a period of fewer legal obligations and fewer interior restraints. Formal discipline will be reduced; all arbitrary intolerance and all absolutism will be abolished. Positive law will be simplified, and the exercise of authority will be moderated. There will be promoted the sense of that Christian freedom which pervaded the first generation of Christians.
>
> General Audience of July 9, 1969. *The Pope Speaks,*
> 4(1969), p. 95.

Yes, today the Church is speaking a new message but it's *new* only when compared to those middle centuries of our history which taught us to think of an impersonal relationship with God. When compared to the early Church — that of the Apostles — it's the same timeless message of Jesus. Thus Vatican II begins to direct the pilgrim people away from an impersonal God and toward a Father who seeks a personal relationship with his children:

> Since Christ in His mission from the Father is the fountain and source of the whole apostolate of the Church, the success of the lay apostolate depends upon the *laity's living union with Christ.* For the Lord has said, ''He who abides in me, and I in him, he bears much

fruit: for without me you can do nothing"
(John 15:5). This life of *intimate union with
Christ* in the Church is nourished by spiritual
aids which are common to all the faithful,
especially active participation in the sacred
liturgy.

Documents of Vatican II, Decree on the Apostolate
of the Laity, #4.

In this chapter we've explored what things can
change in the Church and what forces cause them to
change. We've seen how forces from society can enter
the Church and distort the message of Jesus Christ.
Lastly we've seen Vatican II steer us back on course —
back to a religion based on Jesus' teachings, and to a
Church modeled after the early Church in many vital
respects. And one most important early Church doctrine is our personal relationship with God as Father.
Now we can start to explore the significance and
meaning of such a relationship.

The main point to remember from this chapter is
that the Church is changing traditions which taught us
to relate to God in an impersonal way. The new direction, founded solidly on Scripture and Tradition, is
leading us back to the mainstream. Cardinal Newman
once wrote:

*To live is to change, and to have lived well is
to have changed often.*

CHAPTER 3

The Father's Personalized Pledge

As I walked into Tony's office my eyes became glued to the blackboard. Our jobs as aerospace engineers may be highly technical, but we seldom put such pretentious formulas on our blackboards — usually just sketches of new gadgets to test. "Getting a bit scientific aren't you?" I asked. "Maybe you're trying to impress somebody."

"Oh, the formula," Tony said as he looked up from his desk with an impish grin, "Don't understand it, do you?" His eyes slowly panned across the board reading:

$$\ln \left[\lim_{z \to \infty} \left(1 + \frac{1}{z} \right) \right]^z + (\sin^2 x + \cos^2 x) = \sum_{n=0}^{\infty} \frac{\cosh y \sqrt{1-\tanh^2 y}}{2^n}$$

"No, guess I don't." I was feeling a bit embarrassed now.

"Simple!" Tony replied as he picked up a piece of chalk. "In fact, it's one of the simplest ideas you'll ever come across." The sparkle in his eye and that silly grin told me I'd been had. Very deliberately he wrote beneath the big formula: $1 + 1 = 2$.

"Oh yeah, I recognize it now." At least I thought I did.

Tony leaned back in his chair, still smiling: "Kind of reminds you of Christianity, doesn't it?"

"Ugh . . .?"

"I mean, we make the message of Jesus so complicated. We add on doctrines, talk about sacraments, and dress everything up 'til you can't recognize it anymore." Tony is a dedicated Christian and a very close friend. In fact, he introduced me to a personal relationship with the Father years ago; so once again I had to acknowledge his wisdom.

"You're right, Tony, that's exactly the way it is."

The Father always meant his message to be simple, but men can't leave well enough alone. When Jesus arrived on the scene, he again preached a simple message but men complicated it again. In these next pages we'll discover the beautiful simplicity of Jesus' message — the simple yet hard-to-believe truth about who we are, we who call ourselves Christian.

REBELLION — YET THE PROMISE

No matter how you interpret the Adam and Eve event, its basic message is the same. Man was originally made to enjoy a special relationship with God. The Genesis story says that man and God actually had such a close relationship before man rebelled. Yet rebel he did. Man chose to use his gift of "free will" to act independently. Man was walking in self-sufficiency: walking on a path not chosen by God, or as Vatican II puts it, "finding fulfillment apart from God":

Although he was made by God in a state of holiness, from the very dawn of history man abused his liberty, at the urging of personified Evil. Man set himself against God and sought to find fulfillment apart from God.

Documents of Vatican II, The Church Today, #13.

Man's act of self-sufficiency destroyed that special God-man relationship. It was pure rebellion — pure, because God could not have any fault in himself to cause it. In spite of this rebellion, God would not give up on man for man was the most perfect of all his creations; he would have nothing less than the complete restoration of man's true dignity. But how to do it? Man was now powerless to do it on his own. He lost his power in the rebellion.

Well, God had a plan — a three-step attack on man's pitiful condition. The first step established a principle which shows us the steadfast enduring love of God. *Covenant* is the name we give that principle. You don't have to go very far through Scripture before you find God introducing it: Genesis Chapter 6 is the first place it's mentioned and from that point on in the Bible, covenant is a basic underlying theme. A covenant is a contract or agreement between two people but it's not a contract in the usual sense of the word. You see, it carries with it a sense of permanence, the sense of the two people binding themselves forever in agreement. And this probably will surprise you. When God enters into a covenant, he *binds* himself: actually restricts himself for the sake of his covenant partners. Now God is by nature eternal, so he's binding himself eternally to his covenant partners. The U.S. Bishops emphasized this covenant principle in their ''Basic Teachings'' document:

"The living God" is holy, just, and merciful. Infinitely wise and perfect, he has made *firm commitments* to men and *bound* them to himself by *solemn covenants.* He has each of us always in view. He frees us, saves us, and loves us with the love of a father, the love of a spouse.

Basic Teachings For Catholic Religious Education, #2.

You begin to understand God's love for us (fallen as we are) when you see him enter these eternal agreements. There's no room here for a God who's distant and uncaring. When he enters into a covenant he's saying: "See how much I care for you. I bind myself for your sake; I plan to restore you to dignity." Or as he says in Scripture:

With age-old love I have loved you; so I have kept my mercy toward you.

Jeremiah 31:3

There is one thing more you should understand about covenants: they come in two varieties. Let's call them "conditional" and "unconditional." A conditional covenant simply says, "If you will do 'this and that,' I will do 'thus and so.' " In other words, my promise to you depends upon you fulfilling your part of the agreement. Now as you might suspect, an *un*-conditional covenant contains no such "if" statement. It says, "I will do such and such no matter what happens, no matter what you say or do." Now Scripture reveals that God has entered both types of covenants. Some require you to respond in a certain way; others require only that you accept the covenant. In these unconditional covenants God simply says,

"Here, take it. It's yours."

Now that you understand these basic ideas about covenant, you can look at God's Law and see some remarkable things. First, God promised Moses that he would rescue Israel from Egypt and bring them into the promised land. This fulfilled the *un*conditional covenant he made with Abraham years before. He would do it no matter what the obstacles; and you know the great and unusual things he did to complete that covenant. However, when he gave Moses the Law, God entered a conditional covenant. Much depended upon Israel's faithfully obeying these rules.

> Hear then, Israel, and be careful to observe them, that you may grow and prosper the more.
>
> *Deuteronomy 6:3*

God was telling them their prosperity in the promised land depended directly upon how well they obeyed his Law.

Now it's at this point that many people feel God is becoming a sort of taskmaster, laying down laws and saying, "Obey them or else." But that's not the case at all. God, being the author of human nature, simply was giving man a blueprint of how man was designed to work: he was laying down the principles of operation. In fact, I once heard someone refer to the Bible as "The Manufacturer's Handbook." The law was not so much a "restrictive morality" as it was a plan to live by, a plan in which man could relate to God and to other men properly. When he gave the Law, God clearly stated this point, but too many people have ignored it.

55

> Keep, then, my statues and decrees, for the man who carries them out will *find life* through them.
>
> *Leviticus 18:5*

The law was a loving Father's method of instructing his children on how to find real "life." If God seems harsh and demanding by laying down these rules, you must remember that he was dealing with a rebellious, semi-civilized people who were set in their sinful ways. Giving the Law was really an act of love, and good things were supposed to come from this Law. Moses said:

> As your reward for heeding these decrees and observing them carefully, the Lord, your God, will keep with you the merciful covenant which he promised on oath to your fathers. *He will love and bless and multiply you.*
>
> *Deuteronomy 7:12-13*

But man was weak and fallen and no covenant or law, no matter how perfect, could raise man out of his sinfulness. There had to be still another phase in God's plan before man could be restored. To accomplish this phase, God did the most remarkable and loving thing ever done: he sent Jesus.

THE NEW COVENANT FORETOLD

Some people have mistakenly thought that the "loving God" was only introduced in the New Testament. They talk as if Jesus suddenly sprang the concept of a loving heavenly Father upon an unsuspecting world. However, the Old Testament is full of references to God's love and concern for his people. Through the prophet Hosea the Father spoke these words of love:

> So I will allure her;
> I will lead her into the desert
> and speak to her heart . . .
> I will espouse you to me forever . . .
> in love and in mercy.
>
> *Hosea 2:16, 21*

The ''her'' which God refers to in this passage is Israel. St. Paul points out, however, that Hosea's prophecy was meant to show the Father's love for all people. St. Paul quotes Hosea in Romans, saying:

> Those who were not my people I will call ''my people,'' and those who were not loved I will call ''Beloved.''
>
> *Romans 9:25 (Hosea 2:25)*

In St. Paul's letter to the Corinthians he quotes yet another great prophet, Ezekiel, with the same basic message:

> I will make with them a covenant of peace; it shall be an everlasting covenant with them, and I will multiply them, and put my sanctuary among them forever. My dwelling shall be with them; I will be their God, and they shall be my people.
>
> *Ezekiel 37:26-27 (2 Corinthians 6:16)*

Here we see God talking about a different covenant, a ''new covenant.'' The Father gave another prophet,

Jeremiah, the job of describing exactly what he had in mind. The passage in which Jeremiah proclaims God's message about this "new covenant" is so significant to Christians that the New Testament repeats it completely *(Hebrews 8:8)*. Some theologians have even called it "The Gospel before the Gospel." This is what the Father promised:

> The days are coming, says the Lord, when I will make a new covenant with the house of Israel and the house of Judah. It will not be like the covenant I made with their fathers the day I took them by the hand to lead them forth from the land of Egypt; for they broke my covenant, and I had to show myself their master, says the Lord. But this is the covenant which I will make with the house of Israel after those days, says the Lord. I will place my law within them, and write it upon their hearts; I will be their God, and they shall be my people. No longer will they have need to teach their friends and kinsmen how to know the Lord. All, from least to greatest, shall know me, says the Lord, for I will forgive their evildoing and remember their sin no more.

Jeremiah 31:31-34

To make sure this vital passage would not escape us, the Church Fathers at Vatican II again quote it, and then declare that the "Israel" spoken of is the "New Israel," the Church, which Jesus has instituted.* Since this message is for us who make up the "New Israel," we should take a closer look at it.

The Father begins this prophecy by saying that the

Documents of Vatican II, The Church, #9.

new covenant won't be like the old one. It won't be a set of laws and religious rules given with a stipulation that they will be obeyed or else. No, the new covenant would be quite different. In fact, it would be unlike anything men had ever known. For now God was going to invade men's inner being and "write his law upon their hearts." This was not to be a mere theological concept, because the Father points out that through this process of invasion, men would actually "know the Lord."

Now there is one thing about biblical language that you must understand. When the Scriptures talk about "knowing," they mean much more than head knowledge. They mean knowledge through first-hand experience. So when the Scriptures talk about knowing someone, they mean to know that person through intimate fellowship, even to the extent of knowing how that person thinks and feels. Marital intimacy is a good example of this relationship. So the Father is saying that this new covenant is to be based upon intimate fellowship between man and God. In other words, a powerful new relationship will exist between God the creator and man his creation. He also points out in the last sentence of the prophecy that mercy and forgiveness will be hallmarks of this relationship. In short, man was about to be invaded by the very life, love, mercy and forgiveness of God, but how?

THE NEW COVENANT

This "new covenant" foretold by the prophets was made a reality through one person: Jesus of Nazareth. If you want to understand anything about the covenant, you must look to Jesus Christ. He himself was not the new covenant, but as the prophet

Malachi predicted *(Malachi 3:1)*, Jesus was the "messenger of the covenant." He was to show us the hows and whys of it. He was to show us the beauty and power of it. He was to die that we might partake of it. But the new covenant would only be fulfilled in *us* who would come to believe.

We must agree: Jesus fulfilled his mission perfectly. He constantly told us about the depth, power, beauty and majesty of a new God-man relationship. Let's page through John's Gospel and pick out a few vivid descriptions of this relationship:

I have come in my Father's name *(John 5:43)*. I was sent by One who has the right to send, and him you do not know. I know him because it is from him I come: he sent me *(John 7:28-29)*.

Moreover, the Father who sent me has himself given testimony on my behalf *(John 5:37)*. I am one of those testifying in my behalf, the Father who sent me is the other *(John 8:18)*. If I glorify myself, that glory comes to nothing. He who gives me glory is the Father, the very one you claim for your God, even though you do not know him. But I know him *(John 8:54-55)*.

The Father and I are one. *(John 10:30)* . . . the Father is in me and I in him. *(John 10:38)* . . . no one comes to the Father but through me. If you really knew me, you would know my Father also. From this point on you know him; you have seen him. . . . Whoever has seen me has seen the Father. . . . Do you not believe that I am in the Father and the Father is in me? The words I speak are not spoken of myself; it is the Father who lives in me accomplishing his works. *(John 14:6-10)*

I solemnly assure you, the Son cannot do anything by himself — he can do only what he sees the Father doing. For whatever the Father does, the Son does likewise. For the Father loves the Son and everything the Father does he shows him. *(John 5:19-20)*

. . . I am not alone: I have at my side the One who sent me [the Father]. *(John 8:16)* Father, I thank you for having heard me. I know that you always hear me *(John 11:41-42)*.

In the beginning of John's Gospel Jesus refers to the sacred temple as "my Father's house" *(John 2:16)*. Those words set the theme for John's Gospel. It announces the mystery of a deep and powerful relationship between Jesus and the Father. In the statements you have just read you can clearly see Jesus declaring his total availability to the Father, and in turn the Father pledging total availability to Jesus. Jesus talks about "knowing" the Father. Remember, in biblical language "to know" means "to experience"; so the Father's presence was literally flowing through Jesus. The Father is said to be at Jesus' side and actually teaches him. Jesus expresses a feeling of being "sent" by his Father, and therefore he does whatever the Father wants. Note that Jesus and the Father sense each other's love and respect. Jesus glorifies his Father; the Father in turn glorifies Jesus. So complete is their relationship that finally Jesus has to confess, "The Father and I are one." Yes, they are one in thought, one in purpose, one in mission, one in love for fallen and broken men. You and I don't have to wonder what God must be like. Once you've seen Jesus, really seen him, you've seen the Father. That, of course, is exactly what the Father had in mind.

If you were to ask your friends what God is like, how he acts, how he relates to sinful men, you would get quite a variety of answers. To some he would be the harsh demanding God; to others an all-loving, all-forgiving God. But Christians should have only one answer: *"He's just like Jesus."* That isn't a simplistic answer. On the contrary, it says something really profound. It acknowledges that Jesus was "true God and true man," that he was the true image in the flesh of the invisible I AM. It says that now men have the right to look at Jesus and dare to say they understand what God is like. Incredible, but it comes from the lips of Jesus Christ himself. How merciful is God? How loving? How forgiving? How demanding? How serving? Look at the Gospel of Jesus and you can be sure you know. Jesus said so.

There is one other point you should notice in Jesus' dialogue. The name "Father" is used about eighteen times. "Father" is the name Jesus preferred above all others when talking to (or about) God. To the Hebrews of those days that was a mindblowing revelation. In Jewish history God's name was so sacred that it couldn't be spoken. Now Jesus comes along and refers to the almighty, transcendent I AM simply as "Father." When his disciples ask Jesus how they should pray he says, "This is how you are to pray: 'Our Father . . .' " *(Matthew 6:9)*.

Could it be true? Was he asking mere men to be as familiar with God as he was? Perhaps you've heard Jesus say that too often to really hear it deep in your

heart. It's easy to miss the full impact of that statement, or like the Hebrews of Jesus' day, you may find
his teachings a bit hard to believe. You speak the
words, but deep within you wonder if they could really
be true. But Jesus doesn't stop there; he goes on to
refer to the Father as "Abba" *(Mark 14:36)* and
teaches us to do the same. Jesus' use of this particular
word is significant. Some people might argue that he
meant the word "Father" to be another formal name
for God. In fact, most people use it in just that way.
But Jesus, by introducing "Abba," leaves no room
for such interpretations.

Fr. Brennan Manning* points out that "Abba" is
a word of tender endearment in Hebrew. He notes that
psychologists have discovered something quite significant. The first words spoken by an average American
child one or two years of age are: "Da . . . Da . . . Da
. . . Dada" for Daddy. Now that same child placed in
Israel in Jesus' time would have said: "A . . . A . . . A
. . . Abba." In other words, Abba is equivalent to our
Daddy or Dad. When you use it, you reject any idea of
formality. When Jesus used it, he was telling us just
how intimate this personal relationship would be.

THE UNBELIEVABLE MESSAGE

The way Jesus went about conducting his ministry
should tell you something. Evidently he wasn't trying
to set forth a new philosophy or moral code. If that
were his aim, he would no doubt have selected learned
scribes as his followers instead of fishermen and tax
collectors. He could have even written down instructions himself. But Jesus didn't do that. Why? Because

*Brennan Manning, TOR, author of *The Gentle Revolutionaries* and
Prophets And Lovers.

the last thing he wanted to give the world was a new "religion." It's safe to say that even his closest disciples didn't realize what he was actually up to until his final hours on earth. It took three and a half years' preparation for the disciples, but now Jesus could complete the unbelievable message.

The last supper was the night Jesus tied the loose ends together and told them plainly what his mission was really all about. In effect he said, "I did not come to earth to make better men with better morals. No, I came to make brand new men. The relationship I've enjoyed with my Father is now to be *exactly the same relationship* you're to enjoy."

The new covenant would be a covenant of "Sonship" — God's life invading ordinary men just as it had Jesus. Unbelievable, yes, but it was coming from the One who had lived that relationship for so long. Jesus had said he was the "light of the world."

> While I am in the world I am the light of the world.
>
> *John 9:5*

Now he was saying, "You are the light of the world" *(Matthew 5:14)*. What was his from the Father would now be ours. Jesus was even promising us the same love from the Father that he had known.

> The Father *already loves you,* because you have loved me and have believed that I came from God.
>
> *John 16:27*

Jesus was handing over to us Christians his *total* relationship with the Father; even to the point of the

Father himself giving *us* honor.

> If anyone serves me, him the Father will
> honor.
>
> *John 12:26*

Jesus promises also that the "knowing" or experiencing part of the relationship will be the same:

> A little while now and the world will see me
> no more; but you see me as one who has life,
> and you will have life (divine life). On that day
> *you will know* that I am in my Father, and you
> in me, and I in you. He who obeys the com-
> mandments he has from me is the man who
> loves me; and he who loves me will be loved
> by my Father. I too will love him and *reveal
> myself to him.*
>
> *John 14:19-21*

And what about the many great works Jesus did
while here "in the flesh"? Surely he didn't expect us
to carry on those works! Well, the truth is, he did expect just that. Jesus said:

> I solemnly assure you, the man who has faith
> in me will *do the works I do,* and *greater* far
> than these.
>
> *John 14:12*

Could he really mean it? Jesus knew that men who
had a personal relationship with the Father had that
same abundant power available to them, but not alone.
They needed to be incorporated into a church, a
"body of Christ," to share as Christian brothers that

same power of Jesus.

And the deep, profound joy that Jesus displayed was to be ours too.

> All this I tell you that *my joy may be yours* and your joy may be complete.
>
> *John 15:11*

Now someone might try to argue at this point that Jesus was talking only to his disciples. But that's simply not true. Jesus prayed a powerful prayer for all those who would later be called ''Christians'':

> I do not pray for them alone. I pray also for those who will believe in me through their word, that all may be one as you, Father, are in me, and I in you; I pray that they may be [one] in us, that the world may believe that you sent me. I have *given them the glory you gave me* that they may be one, as we are one — I living in them, you living in me — that their unity may be complete. So shall the world know that you sent me, and that *you loved them as you loved me.*
>
> *John 17:20-23*

Jesus was talking about you and me, ordinary Christians, who were to become *one* in the Father and *one* in the Son. This the Father would do in the third and final step of man's restoration. He would send the Holy Spirit to live within us. It was the Spirit who would implant the divine life and so restore us. Jesus said:

I will ask the Father and he will give you
another Paraclete — to be with you always:
the Spirit of truth, whom the world cannot accept, since it neither sees him nor recognizes
him; but you can recognize him because he remains with you and will be within you.

John 14:16-17

Jesus was not only announcing that God was composed of three divine persons (the Trinity); more
remarkably, he was saying that we were actually going
to partake of the very same life of the Trinity. The
Holy Spirit would make us sons of God — not sons in
the same sense that all men are sons of God, however.
Jesus was saying that we would be sons of God in the
same sense he was. We would have the same divine
life; we would be legitimate sons and daughters of God.

THE SAINTS BELIEVED IT

This belief so permeated the Early Church that St.
Paul triumphantly proclaimed:

All who are led by the Spirit of God are sons of
God. You did not receive a spirit of slavery
leading you back into fear, but a spirit of adop-
tion through which we cry out ''Abba!'' (that
is ''Father''). The Spirit himself gives witness
with our spirit that we are children of God.
But if we are children, we are heirs as well:
heirs of God, heirs with Christ, if only we suf-
fer with him so as to be glorified with him.

Romans 8:14-17

Yes, even ''Abba'' is to be ours. That's how close *our* relationship with the Father is meant to be. But lest anyone think we're misinterpreting Scripture, let's look at the footnote to this passage in the official Catholic translation, *The New American Bible:*

> The Christian, by reason of the Spirit's presence within him, enjoys not only new life but also a *new relationship to God,* that of adopted son and heir through Christ, whose sufferings and glory he shares.
>
> *Footnote to Romans 8:14-17, NAB.*

And this isn't an isolated instance in the writings of St. Paul. Every epistle he wrote proclaims the power of this relationship; Paul made it one of his predominant themes. So let's look at a few more verses. To the Colossians he wrote:

> . . . that mystery hidden from ages and generations past but now revealed to *his holy ones.* God has willed to make known to them the glory beyond price which this mystery brings to the Gentiles — the mystery of *Christ in you.*
>
> *Colossians 1:26-27*

> What you have done is put aside your old self with its past deeds and put on a new man, one who grows in knowledge as he is formed anew in the *image of his Creator.*
>
> *Colossians 3:9-10*

And to the Ephesians:

> This means that you are strangers and aliens no longer. No, you are *fellow citizens* of the saints *and members of the household of God.*
>
> *Ephesians 2:19*

> Be imitators of God as his *dear children.*
>
> *Ephesians 5:1*

Also to the Galatians:

> Each one of you is a *son of God* because of your faith in Christ Jesus.
>
> *Galatians 3:26*

> . . . God sent forth his Son born of a woman, born under the law, to deliver from the law those who were subjected to it, so that we might receive our status as *adopted sons.* The proof that you are sons is the fact that God has sent forth into our hearts the spirit of his Son which cries out ''Abba!'' (''Father!'') You are no longer a slave but a son! And the fact that you are a son makes you an heir, by God's design.
>
> *Galatians 4:4-7*

But St. Paul wasn't the only New Testament writer to proclaim this message. This ''good news'' about the Father raising us to the status of sons and daughters was preached by *all* New Testament writers. For instance:

SAINT JAMES

By his (God's) own choice he made us *his children* by the message of the truth.

James 1:18 (JB)

SAINT JUDE

. . . to those who are called, to those who are *dear to God the Father* and kept safe for Jesus Christ.

Jude 1:1 (JB)

SAINT PETER

As *obedient sons,* do not yield to the desires that once shaped you in your ignorance. Rather, become holy yourselves in every aspect of your conduct, after the likeness of the holy One who called you; remember, Scripture says, ''Be holy, for I am holy.'' In prayer you call upon *a Father* who judges each one justly on the basis of his actions.

1 Peter 1:14-17

SAINT JOHN

What we have seen and heard we proclaim in turn to you so that you may share life with us, this *fellowship of ours is with the Father and with his Son, Jesus Christ.*

1 John 1:3

See what love the Father has bestowed on us in letting us be called *children of God! Yet that is what we are.* . . . we are God's children now; what we shall later be has not yet come to light. We know that when it comes to light we shall be like him, for we shall see him as he is.

1 John 3:1-2

There's one thing to remember here. The epistles of these great men were not directed to canonized saints. They were written to all Christians. They formed basic instructions for those who were new in the faith and also provided guidance for those more mature in the Christian walk. The Church, by proclaiming them part of sacred Scripture, is telling us that their message is for us too.

To demonstrate that this teaching was not confined to the Church of the Apostles, let's move to the fifth century and the writings of St. Leo the Great, Pope of the Roman Catholic Church. We see the message unchanged:

> God our Father has made us his sons and daughters by making us members of his Son's own body. We are not saved on our own; we are saved by being incorporated into Jesus Christ.

Anne Field, O.S.B., *Binding of the Strong Man*, p. 55.

In another place St. Leo exhorts Christians to praise and thank our Father . . .

> . . . for the inexpressible love of our Lord in becoming man for us, changing our guilt into innocence and making our old sin-burdened nature new. We see strangers becoming the *adopted children of God* and outsiders entering upon the inheritance of sons, sinners beginning to be holy.

Ibid., p. 34.

Let's step across the centuries again and see what Vatican II had to say. The documents are literally full of references to our relationship with the Father and Jesus. Here are just a few:

> Therefore, by divine condescension the laity have Christ for their *brother* who, though He is the Lord of all, came not to be served but to serve.
>
> *Documents of Vatican II*, The Church, #32.

> The Church holds that the recognition of God is in no way hostile to man's dignity, since this dignity is rooted and perfected in God. For man was made an intelligent and free member of society by the God who created him. *Even more importantly, man is called as a son to commune with God* and to share in His happiness.
>
> *Documents of Vatican II*, The Church Today, #21.

> We believe that the Father so loved the world that He gave His own Son to save it. Indeed, through this same Son of His He freed us from bondage to sin, reconciling all things unto Himself through Him, ''making peace through the blood of his cross,'' so that ''we might be called *sons of God, and truly be such.*''
>
> *Documents of Vatican II*, Message to Humanity.

We could follow this teaching with absolute continuity throughout the centuries. Why? Because it's at the very heart of Jesus' message. In Chapter 2 we saw how the culture of certain centuries distorted or misinterpreted the message, but the message itself has never changed — nor will it ever change. If we or Christians of any other century have not heard or understood this message, it's not because it wasn't there. It has always had a prominent place in the official teachings and theology of the Church. A few great Christians of every century have heard the message and have found the "Father," and they've always said that the relationship they enjoyed should be experienced by everyone. Somehow we didn't hear them. It was always a message for someone else. Today we Christians must grasp the message and discover who we are. Cardinal Suenens has expressed it this way:

> What is lacking in us is a realization of our Christian identity. We dare not believe with an expectant faith that the various gifts of the Spirit are always there for the Church of God. We do not recall often enough that we are rich with the riches of God and that these are ours in faith for the humble asking if we are ready to receive them with confidence. We Christians do not know who we are. *We are children of God,* heirs to his Kingdom, but we behave as if it were not so. We have at our disposal spiritual treasures which remain buried because their existence is unknown to us, or because we lack the faith to believe that they can be found and used.
>
> *A New Pentecost?*, p. 110.

Yes, Jesus established the New Covenant so that we, fallen and sinful, might be restored to the Father as sons and daughters. The new covenant gives us identity in Jesus Christ — now we can truly know who we are. And even more remarkable, this covenant is unconditional — we don't have to do anything to deserve it. The covenant is signed in the blood of Jesus by the Father who can be trusted to carry it out. It's a covenant of life, the life of the Trinity in us that makes us (in a real, true, concrete sense) sons and daughters of the Father.

Fantastic!

Thank you Father, for we could never have guessed what you had in store for us.

CHAPTER 4

Who Would Believe What We Have Heard?

If this idea seems hard to believe — the Father having the same relationship with you that he had with Jesus — then I must confess something. That relationship implies some other equally hard-to-believe things concerning your everyday life.

Now I can't explain everything in a single chapter: a good treatment would take volumes. But I can list a few important ''what's and how's'' of this hard-to-believe relationship. For instance:

1. What is the Father's life going to do in you?
2. How deep is the Father's love for you personally?
3. What does it mean to be holy?
4. How do you come to really ''know'' the Father as Father?
5. What will this relationship do for your self-awareness?

Unless you understand these things, you'll never understand what it means to be Christian. For in saying that you are Christian, you're essentially admitting that you've already begun to experience some kind of personal relationship with the Father; the two go hand in hand. When your understanding of the relationship is weak, your Christianity is weak. That's why you as a Christian should be keenly aware that the Father is a personal, loving God. Christian life without this personal relationship makes no sense at all. Cardinal Suenens has said:

> . . . God has meaning only if he is the living and personal God.
>
> *A New Pentecost?*, p. 124.

So let's answer these questions and find out what this relationship implies for you and me.

THE REMAKING OF MAN

For many people, Jesus is only a spiritual lifeguard who throws the drowning sinner a life preserver and pulls him into heaven. Jesus, however, saw his mission quite differently. He was not so much interested in getting fallen men out of hell and into heaven, as he was to get God out of heaven and into men. Vatican II clearly stated this principle when it said:

> In His goodness and wisdom, God chose to reveal Himself and to make known to us the hidden purpose of His will . . . by which through Christ, the Word made flesh, *man has access to the Father in the Holy Spirit and comes to share in the divine nature* . . . Through this revelation, therefore, the invisible God . . . out of the abundance of His love speaks to men *as friends* . . . and lives among them, so that He may invite and take them

into *fellowship* with Himself.

Documents of Vatican II, Dogmatic Constitution
on Divine Revelation, #2.

But fellowship with the Father isn't the only goal. As I said before, the Father created us originally as an image of himself. Our original human nature had great beauty and dignity. But when man rebelled, he defaced that dignity; he cheapened it. Fallen man is much less than he was meant to be, for man was designed to act as a mirror of God's own glory. Fallen man has the potential to be a beautiful example of the Father's creative ability, but the only way he can achieve that potential is through letting Jesus Christ put divine life back into him. Saint Leo the Great expressed it in this way:

> If we think for a while about God's plan for the creation of the human race and the way he has made us in his own image, we begin to understand that we are meant to be like a mirror reflecting his likeness in all its beauty and goodness.

Anne Field, O.S.B., *The Binding of the Strong Man,* p. 23.

And he goes on to say:

> But we must recognize the dignity of our human nature. We were made in the image of God, an image which was indeed defaced in Adam, but which has been *restored in Christ.*

Ibid., p. 35.

In other words Jesus came to ''save'' us through this restoration process. He came to give us new life —

divine life. He came to raise us up from sin into the abundance of God himself. Jesus said:

> I came that they might have life and have it to the full.

John 10:10

Now exactly why did the Father want to remake us? Let's look at some practical examples. Have you ever made something with your own hands — a thing you were quite pleased with — and then have it tragically defaced? Immediately you want to restore it to its original beauty. Or have you ever seen a child at play — running, jumping, laughing? Suddenly the child stumbles, falls and comes crying to you with skinned knees and tear-filled eyes. You immediately want to restore the child to his original happiness. Well then, you shouldn't have any trouble understanding how the Father felt when he looked upon man, his most perfect creation, and saw him fallen from dignity and beauty. The Father longed to restore man to his original perfection. Only he knows how beautiful that really was. To accomplish this restoration, the Father needed to take man from the Kingdom of Darkness (into which he had fallen) and place him in the Kingdom of Light.

So when Jesus said ''enter the Kingdom,'' he was not inviting you to heaven some time in the future. He was asking you to enter the Kingdom of God present on earth *here and now.* Jesus said the Kingdom of God was not this place called heaven, but rather an *experience* of the Father's life in your inmost being. His words were:

. . . the Kingdom of God is *within* you.

Luke 17:21 (KJV)

The invitation to enter the ''Kingdom'' is an invitation to experience God's life and God's love within you now. As Cardinal Suenens has said:

> He invites all of us to *experience,* even here below, the warmth of his love; he has made us just for that.

A New Pentecost?, p. 69.

St. Peter wrote to the Christians of his day telling them that they were '' . . . sharers of the divine nature'' *(2 Peter 1:4).* Yes, when you receive the Father's life within, you actually start to take on his own divine nature. Again let me stress an important point. The Father's aim is not to change men into better men with better morals; his plan is to completely change our nature. C.S. Lewis once wrote:

> It is not a change from brainy men to brainier men: it is a change that goes off in a totally different direction — a change from being creatures of God to being sons of God.

Mere Christianity, p. 185.

Now I think you can understand why ''religious experience'' must be a part of this personal relationship. If a person truly allows that divine life to enter him and start to remake him, it has to be felt. God is going to be *experienced* in a very real way. Cardinal Suenens pointed to a teaching of one of the greatest intellectual men of all time:

St. Thomas Aquinas, a theologian whom no one would suspect of anti-intellectualism, teaches that the object of faith is not found in doctrinal propositions concerning God, but in God himself *known and loved in a personal relationship.*

A New Pentecost?, p. 57.

You can see that this "remaking of man" is no mere theological concept. It is, in fact, a genuine restoration to man's original dignity through which he enters the Kingdom of God here and now. It's an infusion of divine life which, when it comes, starts to change the sinful human nature into a divine nature; and most important, it's a dynamic event that will be experienced as the Father is known in a personal relationship.

A FATHER'S LOVE

Another important reason for receiving this divine life is that you might actually experience "real" love — the Father's love. We talked about the Father's love in a somewhat general way in the last chapter, now you need to see it as something directed personally to you. If you understand the Father's putting his life into you *only* to restore your dignity, you miss an essential point. "God *is* love" according to St. John *(1 John 4:8).* His very nature is love. St. John prefaced the quote above by saying,

The man without love has known nothing of God. . . .

1 John 4:8

In other words, St. John says that the thing which makes God exist is simply ''to love''; therefore you can't understand the Father's actions until you understand his love and begin to return it. Jesus himself said:

> Yes, God so loved the world that he gave his only Son.
>
> *John 3:16*

When you see the Father giving Jesus to this world, you begin to understand his love. To love is to give of yourself, and the Father gave of himself perfectly when he gave his only begotten Son. In turn, Jesus was the perfect reflection of the Father's love. For he gave all he had to give — his very life. He gave up the richness of heaven to become poor for you, as St. Paul says:

> You are well acquainted with the favor shown you by our Lord Jesus Christ; how for your sake he made himself poor though he was rich, so that you might become rich by his poverty.
>
> *2 Corinthians 8:9*

If you were already a good and holy person you might understand the Father sacrificing his beloved Son. But, St. Paul says:

> It is precisely in this that God *proves his love* for us: that while we were *still sinners,* Christ died for us.
>
> *Romans 5:8*

Yes, the Father loves his people with a merciful love, a love that overlooks our sinfulness and sees our potential as sons and daughters. The U.S. Bishop's "Basic Teachings" document proclaims:

> One must have toward God the attitude of a son to an all-good, *all loving Father,* and must never think or live as if independent of God.
>
> *Basic Teachings for Catholic Religious Education, #*19.

Many recent surveys of young Catholics show that our teenagers relate to a Jesus who shows love and compassion, but God the Father still remains distant, unknowable and somewhat on the cold side when it comes to "love." And there's usually no understanding at all of the Holy Spirit. These teenagers, I believe, mirror the thoughts and attitudes of most modern Catholics. Somehow they've dissected the Trinity, giving the Father all the authority, Jesus all the love and the Holy Spirit only white feathers. Through mental laziness they forget quite conveniently that God is "One." It challenges the mind to think that the three persons of the Trinity have a oneness of purpose, a oneness of love, a oneness of mercy. People fail to see that *love* is the dynamic nature of the Trinity. Yes, love is the very lifeblood of the Father, Son and Holy Spirit. If Jesus is seen as a loving, compassionate, merciful God, then the Father must be seen in exactly the same way. Remember, Jesus came to show men (and to give them) the Father's own love. He prayed:

> To them I have revealed your name, and I will continue to reveal it so that *your love* for me *may live in them,* and I may live in them.
>
> *John 17:26*

The love which Jesus knew so well, the Father's love that sustained him through so many trials, the love that motivated him to accept the cross — yes, that very same love is being offered to you and me.

Jesus was constantly trying to make people understand the Father's love, only to find them locked into thought patterns that were centuries old — thought patterns that simply could not see God, creator of the universe, and God, loving Father, at the same time. Finally Jesus gave the perfect description of this loving Father when he gave us the Parable of the Prodigal Son. It's by no means just a nice story of a father-son reunion after adolescent folly. No, you have to put yourself into the heart of that story. Jesus wants *you* to become the prodigal. And like the prodigal, you must approach the Father and say: "Father, I want to do my own thing. Let me exercise my inheritance of a free will. Let me give this world a spin or two. After I've done my thing I'll come back and see you." And so, with saddened eyes, the Father lets you go. It's known as permissive love. The Father knows all too well what lies ahead, but there's no telling the prodigal; you're too headstrong to listen. Off you go, off for fun, adventure, power, pleasure, riches and anything else that will give you what you're really after — happiness.

It may take a short time, as in the case of the prodigal son, or many long years of search, but eventually you'll find there's no genuine, lasting happiness in those glittering idols the world offers. No matter what path you might have taken to find worldly happiness, you can be sure that somewhere along the way sin was involved. Jesus knew it would be that way. He knew, like the prodigal, that you would finally decide (if you're honest with yourself) that you must return to the Father. And it's at this point that people usually make the same mistake the prodigal makes. He reasons that even the second-class members of his father's household, the slaves and hired hands, are far better off than he is at the present time. "Perhaps if I compose a nice speech of repentance and show my father that I know how wrong I was . . . perhaps then he'll let me be his slave," thinks the prodigal.

Jesus now puts in the surprising twist to the parable. Up to now things have gone along as you might expect they would. But Jesus points out the unexpected nature of the father. He describes how the father has more than a casual interest in his son's returning, in spite of all the son had done. The father watches for his son's return constantly and when he finally sees him (still far away) the father runs out to meet him. Upon reaching his son, the father embraces and kisses the prodigal who is somewhat stunned by all this. Nevertheless, the son begins to recite his well-prepared speech of repentance, sorrow, and guilt:

> "Father, I have sinned against God and against you; I no longer deserve to be called your son."
>
> *Luke 15:21*

The father, however, seems not to hear any of it. His son is home and nothing else matters. He interrupts the son's speech by shouting directions to the servants:

> "Quick! bring out the finest robe and put it on him; put a ring on his finger and shoes on his feet. Take the fatted calf and kill it. Let us eat and celebrate because this son of mine was dead and has come back to life. He was lost

and is found." Then the celebration began.

Luke 15:22-24

Do you really hear what Jesus is saying to you through this parable? The father knew what his son had done: how he had wasted his money, fallen into sin and disgraced his father's name. Yet this father was somehow able to overlook all that. He loved his son with a merciful, forgiving love that didn't require great speeches of repentance, only a sincere heart. The ring on the prodigal's finger and the shoes on his feet meant that he was being restored to *sonship* and nothing less.

Jesus is asking you, through his parable, to try to grasp another hard-to-believe truth: that God our heavenly Father reacts in the very same way whenever you come to him with your life full of wasted talents, plunged in sin and giving glory only to yourself. Jesus is telling you not to limit the Father's mercy and love for you to your own puny concept of what merciful love is. Our Father is far beyond that. In Hosea the Father declares:

"For I am God and not man."

Hosea 11:9

You must never limit the Father's love and forgiveness to the kind you've understood or experienced as a human being. You see, God is love and it matters not whether you can imagine the Father being in love with you. Your concept of his love has been distorted by your own sins and the sins of others. His concept of love is not distorted. He clearly stated through Jesus that he is a loving Father. Your feelings about yourself have to take a back seat to that unalterable truth. Cardinal Suenens writes:

> In the pages of the Old Testament and the
> New, God speaks to me today. I should there-
> fore receive his words as I would the letter of a
> friend who shares with me all my cares, fears
> and hopes, who walks at my side, showing me
> the way.
>
> *A New Pentecost?*, p. 38.

As a Christian you can never in truth think of
yourself as being unloved. To say that the Father
doesn't love you *personally* is a lie, and nothing short
of that. St. Paul in his letter to the Romans triumphantly declares:

> For I am certain that neither death nor life,
> neither angels nor principalities, neither the
> present nor the future, nor powers, neither
> height nor depth nor any other creature, will
> be able to separate us from the love of God
> that comes to us in Christ Jesus, our Lord.
>
> *Romans 8:38-39*

Yes, the Father loves each of us in an intimate, personal way. He loves with a love that forgives all sin, no
matter how serious. As St. Leo said:

> Everything he does for us *proves his fatherly
> love.*
>
> Anne Field, O.S.B., *The Binding of the Strong Man,* p. 24.

If you believe anything less than this total, consuming
love for you personally, you've esentially rejected
Jesus' message and the ''New Covenant'' purchased

by his blood. If you seek this personal relationship, you must sincerely seek to know the Father's love. You must seek to *experience* its fullness.

Remember the Father's words:

Can a mother forget her infant, be without tenderness for the child of her womb? Even should she forget, I will never forget you.

Isaiah 49:15

A GIFT CALLED HOLINESS

You might think the Father's love would be all you need. But he wants even more for you. He wants to bring you into the "Family" as a full-fledged member. To do that he'll ask you to take on some characteristics of the Family, especially the one called "holiness."

Now I want to explain a few things about this idea of holiness. To the average Catholic the idea of being holy is somewhat unreal. We just don't think that way. The reason we don't is what I like to call "sloppy theology." You see, everyone has some vague idea of what holiness is (or ought to be), but we seldom "think it out." Because of this, there are too many misconceptions and plain old untruths going around about holiness. We're a lot like Peter who saw that Jesus was holy, and falling on his knees, pleaded:

Leave me, Lord. I am a sinful man.

Luke 5:8

All too often we haven't heard what Jesus said in reply:

Do not be afraid.

Luke 5:10

Yes, most of us are afraid when confronted with the holiness of God. We know (or think we know) that such holiness is impossible for us. "Leave such matters to the priests and nuns. Life is hard enough as it is," we retort. Well, that answer points all the more to our lack of understanding. You see, a personal relationship with the Father is tied in with this whole idea of holiness.

Vatican II was aware of these many misconceptions and set out to clear the air. It spoke quite often about our call to holiness.

> The lord Jesus, the divine Teacher and Model of all perfection, preached *holiness* of life to each and every one of His disciples, regardless of their situation: "You therefore are to be perfect, even as your heavenly Father is perfect" (Matthew 5:48).
>
> *Documents of Vatican II,* The Church, #40.

> The New Testament texts cited in this article make it evident that not only those who live according to the evangelical counsels but *all Christians* are called to "the fullness of the Christian life and to the perfection of charity." It would be an error to think of *holiness* as the special preserve of some one class of Christians, e.g., the religious.
>
> Footnote from Vatican II Documents for the reference above.

The Council Fathers, therefore, made it clear: no matter what a person's situation in life, if he claims to be a Christian, he's called to holiness. There's no "passing the buck" to those dedicated to the religious life. Priests, nuns and others in religious life simply have a different route to take in getting there. The Council Fathers stated bluntly that all of us are *equal* in Christian dignity and therefore are *equal* in our call to holiness.

> Therefore, the chosen People of God is one: "one Lord, one faith, one baptism" . . . As members, they share a common dignity from their rebirth in Christ. . . . If therefore everyone in the Church does not proceed by the same path, nevertheless *all are called to sanctity* and have received an *equal* privilege of faith through the justice of God . . . And if by the will of Christ some are made teachers, dispensers of mysteries, and shepherds on behalf of others, yet all share a *true equality* with regard to the dignity . . . of the Body of Christ.
>
> *Documents of Vatican II,* The Church, #32.

What Vatican II said was this: there are many different pathways to holiness (laity, priesthood, sisterhood, contemplatives, etc.) but the very *same* holiness is obtained by all. You might think of it as multitudes of people traveling to a great city. Some go by plane, some by bus, some by train and some by car — but no matter what means they use to get there, their destination is the same.

> In the various types and duties of life, one and the *same* holiness is cultivated by all who are moved by the Spirit of God.
>
> *Documents of Vatican II,* The Church, #41.

Therefore, in the Catholic Church it matters not whether you're a lay person or religious, of the hierarchy or served by it, you're called to the same holiness and that's all there is to it.

> He (Jesus) united her (the Church) to Himself as His own body and crowned her with the gift of the Holy Spirit, for God's glory. Therefore in the Church, *everyone* belonging to the hierarchy, or being cared for by it, is *called to holiness,* according to the saying of the Apostle: "For this is the will of God, your sanctification."
>
> *Documents of Vatican II,* The Church, #39.

At this point I am quite sure you're willing to admit that the Father and his Church are calling everyone to holiness, but at the same time you're perplexed about why and how you yourself are called. Most of these problems arise because we really don't understand exactly what holiness is. We've dressed up our ideas with all sorts of pious pictures and virtuous notions. Most of these are distortions of the real picture. So we need to throw away all our old misconceptions about holiness and seek the truth.

If you studied the whole Bible and were attentive enough, you'd notice that holiness is treated differently in the Old Testament than in the New Testament. The Old Testament looks at holiness as part of God's nature. The ordinary man can't approach that holiness. God is holy; man is something else. Many people today have this Old Testament holiness in mind when they read about their "call to holiness" and simply despair from the start. They know they can never be *that* holy, and of course they're quite right.

But the New Testament holiness is somewhat different, and you as a Christian should understand how it's different.

First of all, holiness doesn't mean "perfection." Vatican II said:

> For even now on this earth the Church is marked with a *genuine* though *imperfect holiness.*
>
> *Documents of Vatican II,* The Church, #48.

If you're waiting to become perfect to be declared holy, you've got a long wait ahead. To be holy you don't have to be perfect. If you're thinking otherwise, you're thinking like a Pharisee.

> When the scribes who belonged to the Pharisee party saw that he was eating with tax collectors and offenders against the law, they complained to his disciples, "Why does he eat with such as these?" Overhearing the remark, Jesus said to them, "People who are healthy do not need a doctor; sick people do. I have come to call sinners, not the self-righteous."
>
> *Mark 2:16-17*

Jesus was holy, but the Pharisees couldn't see his holiness because he associated with sinners. Yes, God our Father chose sinners as the first to receive his new life. They weren't the ones who appeared holy (like the Pharisees), but ordinary everyday sinners like you and me. You see, the Father's new life — the life which makes us holy — is so valuable that we can't even earn it. Nothing anyone could do would be

91

enough to merit this new life. So the Father demonstrated this principle by first giving his new life to people who clearly were not holy before they received it. Jesus' small army of followers was composed of former tax collectors (traitors to their countrymen), former prostitutes, plus all sorts of ordinary people whom nobody would consider holy. With such disciples, Jesus demonstrated what a great love the Father had for the ordinary person. The Father didn't demand that they be holy first. As St. Paul says:

> For our sakes *God made* him who did not know sin to be sin, so that in him *we might become* the very holiness of God.
>
> 2 Corinthians 5:21

I think you can see now why holiness is one of the most misunderstood concepts in Christianity today. I've already said that it isn't being perfect, it isn't something you can earn, and you don't have to be a saint to get it. But exactly what *is* it?

The New Testament term "holiness" is used interchangeably with another word: *sanctification.* So you can get a clear definition of New Testament holiness by closely examining the meaning of "sanctification." Now some theologians have dressed up this word with high sounding descriptions also, but its basic meaning is really quite simple. To "sanctify" something is to set it apart for the intelligent purpose for which it was intelligently designed. In this context you can sanctify anything. For instance, you can sanctify your shoes by putting them on your feet and walking in them. Of course you could also put them on your hands in place of gloves. That might work, but you wouldn't be sanctifying the shoes because it wasn't the intelligent purpose for which they were made. Also, people would no doubt think you were a bit odd. Shoes were meant to be put on feet and be walked in — to do so is, in a sense, to sanctify them.

Now let's put this principle of sanctification into a religious context. To be sanctified means to be *set apart* by the Father for the intelligent purpose for which he intelligently made you. And that purpose is fellowship with him through sonship. The Father's life entering you sets you apart: apart from Satan's kingdom of darkness, apart from worldly values, apart from death itself. To be sanctified (or made holy), therefore, is to be joined to the "People of God," a people he has chosen to proclaim his Kingdom here on earth. Thus St. Peter wrote:

> . . . you are *a chosen race, a royal priesthood, a consecrated nation, a people set apart* to sing the praises of God who called you out of the darkness into his wonderful light. Once you were *not a people* at all and now you are the People of God.
>
> *1 Peter 2:9-10 (JB)*

It's important to see that only when the Father's life enters you, and not before, do you become holy. Yet that holiness has entered a sinful vessel. Therefore, the moment the divine life enters, the Father starts you out on a journey. It's a journey to *greater* sanctification. Our whole Christian life is supposed to be a continual, step-by-step growth in being "set apart" for the Father. Saint Paul told the Thessalonians:

It is God's will that you *grow in holiness:* that
you abstain from immorality.

You might think of it like this: the Father's life
entering you could be likened to his planting a rose
bush covered with small unopened buds. He can see
the potential beauty in those buds while you probably
cannot. But the Father knows that with patient gentle
care the plant will grow stronger and healthier until
one day the buds burst forth into sunlight with radiant
beauty. Thus the expression: "Bloom where you're
planted." Now some people act as if they must do the
planting and they think the bush must be in full bloom
of holiness before the Father will be pleased. But our
Father says, "No, I'll do the planting, watering and
pruning. All you have to do is open up to my
sunlight." How you open up to the Father's sunlight
is a topic for a later chapter.

If this idea of "imperfect holiness" still bothers
you, think of it in terms of baking a loaf of bread. You
put the loaf in the oven knowing that it takes thirty
minutes to be completely finished. So you don't get
upset when, after only fifteen minutes, you look in and
notice it's only half-baked. It isn't supposed to be
done! In the same way, the Father starts you "cook-
ing" when his new life enters. When he looks at you
and sees that you aren't quite done (aren't completely
holy), he doesn't get upset. He knows you need more
time. In this sense you could say that we're all "half-
baked Christians."

I hope you can see now that receiving God's life is
simply not an end in itself. The Father has placed it
there for the primary purpose of its growing stronger
and stronger until:

> . . . we will be able to arrive at perfect union
> with Christ, that is, holiness.
>
> *Documents of Vatican II,* The Church, #50.

Now it's logical to think of perfect holiness as being a long way off. For most of us it is just that. But if you stop where you are in your Christian journey, if you decide that you've grown enough for now, you'll begin to die. If you hesitate for too long, your buds of holiness will completely die off and then you'll become just a dried out thorn bush. To stop in your Christian walk is, in fact, to say no. "No, I won't follow you." To accept your present level of spirituality and be content with it is to no longer follow Jesus Christ and his Church. For the Fathers of that Church have identified us as a pilgrim people, a people on the move, a people moving on to greater holiness.

> All of Christ's followers, therefore, are invited
> and *bound to pursue holiness* and the perfect
> fulfillment of their proper state.
>
> *Documents of Vatican II,* The Church, #42.

Holiness is not an option for a true Christian. The Catholic Church declares that we are *bound* to pursue it. The Laity are specifically told to . . .

> . . . *make progress in holiness* . . .
>
> *Documents of Vatican II,* Decree on the Apostolate
> of the Laity, #4.

So you can see that the moment you're baptized, the Father's special life enters you and sets you apart as one of *his* people. At the same time you're asked to make that newfound holiness grow. Cardinal Suenens writes:

The Spirit of God is in a baptized person. The promise of God is accomplished; the Christian soul is a dwelling place of the Blessed Trinity. Consequently holiness is not a long climb toward some far off and inaccessible peak. Christian sanctity is given from the very beginning. Strictly speaking we have not to become holy, but to remain so: we must become what we already are.

A New Pentecost?, pp. 83-84.

Let's not forget those words, ''We must become what we already are.''

TO KNOW AND BE KNOWN

As I said before, through this personal relationship you'll begin to ''know'' the Father as father. Let's look a bit deeper into that truth. If I were to ask you how many people you know, you'd most likely list dozens. But then, if I said, ''How many people do you really know?'', you'd reflect a bit perhaps and say, ''If you mean in the sense of knowing their feelings and inner thoughts, I guess only a few.'' And, of course, that's true of almost everyone. You know *many* people in the sense that you have, through some intellectual process, collected facts about them. You can list their age, occupation, habits, likes and dislikes. Yet you can know all sorts of things about them, and not really know them. Those few people you ''know'' in the sense of knowing their interior personality are limited to your close friends, relatives and spouse. You know not only facts about them, but you have actually experienced them through personal relationships. You know what they think about various things and how they will react in a given situation.

So there are two different ways in which you can talk about ''knowing'' someone. You might break it down like this:

KNOWING (Intellectual)	KNOWING (Through Experience)
Facts gathered by the mind (i.e. ''head knowledge'')	Facts gathered by the mind *plus* actual experience of personal relationships (i.e. head *plus* heart knowledge)

Now the Scriptures talk a great deal about ''knowing God,'' but many people believe the Scriptures mean intellectual knowledge. The kind of knowledge you'd get by studying George Washington or Abraham Lincoln. That concept, as I pointed out earlier, is completely false. The Scriptures were written in a Hebrew society which didn't have a concept of knowing ''intellectually.'' In fact, they didn't even have a word for intellectual knowledge. When the Scriptures talk about knowing God, there can be no mistaking the meaning. To ''know God'' in the scriptural sense is to experience him through a personal, intimate relationship and nothing short of that. Therefore, when St. John says:

> We have come to *know* and to believe in the love God has for us.
>
> *1 John 4:16*

or when St. Paul says:

> I have come to rate all as loss in the light of the surpassing *knowledge* of my Lord Jesus Christ.
>
> *Philippians 3:8*

they are speaking of a real, concrete *experience* of the Father's love for them personally. This relationship isn't a one way street. Love and knowledge flow in both directions. James the Apostle wrote:

> Draw close to God, and he will draw close to you.
>
> *James 4:8*

and St. Paul adds:

> Now that you have come to know God — or rather, have been known by him — how can you return to those powerless, worthless, natural elements?
>
> *Galatians 4:9*

So a "knowing relationship" means you'll combine head knowledge and heart knowledge into a real sense of knowing how the Father feels about things in your life. In short, you'll begin to "put on" the mind of God.

Obviously it's impossible for you, using your human strength and intellect, to ever accomplish such a knowing relationship on your own. You'll need help. Now Jesus had this knowing relationship and he promised that all Christians would also have it. Through Jesus' sacrifice you've been given an injection of divine life, and it's that life which makes this knowing relationship possible. As St. Paul says:

> May the God of our Lord Jesus Christ, the Father of glory, grant you a spirit of wisdom and insight to *know* him clearly.
>
> *Ephesians 1:17*

Remember that the spirit of wisdom which the Father gives helps you to "know" him in the biblical sense. It doesn't make you a smarter person in the worldly sense. The knowledge the world gives through education may be valuable; then again it may not. St. Paul warned that intellectual knowledge alone can create problems.

> Stay clear of worldly, idle talk and the contradictions of what is falsely called knowledge. In laying claim to such knowledge, some men have missed the goal of faith.
>
> *1 Timothy 6:20-21*

So the wisdom you're after in your quest for God is a spiritual wisdom. It's just as wise as any worldly, intellectual knowledge, but it has a special purpose: to know the Father's will. St. Paul explained this to the Colossians:

> Ever since we heard this we have been praying for you unceasingly and asking that you may attain *full knowledge of his will* through perfect wisdom and spiritual insight. Then you will lead a life worthy of the Lord and pleasing to him in every way. You will multiply good works of every sort and grow in the *knowledge of God.*
>
> *Colossians 1:9-10*

You've seen that Jesus was more than just a great religious leader. He was totally involved in this unique and never before known relationship with the Father. He was the Father's living example of what men ought to be. So if you want to understand just how deep your own "knowing" relationship will become with the Father, you have to look at Jesus and his relationship with the Father. Remember, Jesus said that you're to have exactly the *same* relationship.

One of Jesus' favorite illustrations of the knowing relationship was the image of shepherd and sheep. Now sheep are certainly not the smartest of domesticated animals. Still they "know" their shepherd. If you saw two shepherds come together for a chat, you'd notice their two herds mingling and to all appearances there would be only one large herd. But when the shepherds separated again, the sheep belonging to each shepherd would follow only their master. They "know" which shepherd he is, not by intellectual reasoning, but by experience. So Jesus establishes clearly the kind of relationship and knowledge that Christians are to expect. He said:

> I am the good shepherd. I *know* my sheep and my sheep *know* me in the *same way* that the Father *knows* me and I *know* my Father.
>
> *John 10:14-15*

The Jerusalem Bible is noted for its excellent footnotes which provide the reader with a running commentary on the Scriptures by noted Catholic scholars. The Jerusalem Bible footnote for the passage above states:

> In biblical language . . . "knowledge" is not merely the conclusion of an intellectual process, but the fruit of an *"experience,"* a *personal contact;* . . . when it matures, it is love.

To know and be known — that's the message of Jesus. To know the Father through Jesus exactly as

Jesus knew the Father — that's the message of salvation. It's hard to believe that the Father could care for you with such intimate, personal love. Yet you have the words of Jesus who said:

> Are not two sparrows sold for next to nothing? Yet not a single sparrow falls to the ground without *your* Father's consent. As for you, every hair of your head has been counted; so do not be afraid of anything.
>
> *Matthew 10:29-31*

It's at this point that many people have a problem grasping the reality of the message. "Surely he couldn't mean that literally," they exclaim. "There are simply too many people for the Father to know each one personally." Yet the sacred Scriptures state clearly that it's so. People relying on human reason, however, find it too much to handle. They fail to see that God is not bound by the feeble constraints of human reason. Short-sighted men with short-sighted reason have always found the Father's ways hard to contend with. C.S. Lewis spoke of the Father's personal care, saying:

> He does not have to deal with us in the mass. You are as much alone with Him as if you were the only being He had ever created. When Christ died, He died for you individually just as much as if you had been the only man in the world.
>
> *Mere Christianity*, p. 147.

If that's true — and it is — how can God ever find the time to listen to you when there are so many people trying to get through? Well, that's a valid question. But in asking it, you automatically assume that God is restricted to ''time'' the same way you are. I've come to believe, as did C.S. Lewis, that God is in fact outside time, since it was he who created it in the first place. C.S. Lewis put it this way:

> If you picture Time as a straight line along which we have to travel, then you must picture God as the whole page on which the line is drawn. We come to the parts of the line one by one: we have to leave A behind before we get to B, and cannot reach C until we leave B behind. God, from above or outside or all around, contains the whole line, and sees it all.
>
> *Mere Christianity*, p. 147.

In this example the Father merely takes that part of the line which makes up your life and moves it over to a section of the page (which contains all eternity) and there studies it in detail. You see, in the space of eternity there is plenty of time for your individual needs. Thus the great King David wrote:

> O Lord, you have probed me and you know me;
> you know when I sit and when I stand;
> you understand my thoughts from afar.
> My journeys and my rest you scrutinize,
> with all my ways you are familiar.
> Even before a word is on my tongue,
> behold, O Lord, you know the whole of it.
>
> *Psalm 139:1-4*

So now you have a concept which helps you understand how the Father, who is outside of time, can see the whole of your life from beginning to end in a single glance. He can take any moment in your life and, in the expanse of his time-frame (which has no limits), examine it in minute detail. If such personal attention seems hard to believe, you must remember that as a Christian you have no choice but to believe it; Jesus taught that it was so. He spoke the message clearly, a message of personal love and concern:

Stop worrying, then, over questions like, ''What are we to eat, or what are we to drink, or what are we to wear?'' The unbelievers are always running after these things. Your heavenly Father *knows all that you need.*

Matthew 6:31-32

You must constantly remind yourself that Jesus was speaking the Father's words, thinking the Father's thoughts, doing the Father's will:

. . . and whoever looks on me is seeing him who sent me.

John 12:45

I think you can see that there are many people today — Christians and non-Christians alike — who know *about* God, but don't actually *know* him. It doesn't matter how faithfully you perform your religious duties, or how ''good'' you are, or how much the Holy Spirit is supposed to be working through you. Jesus placed all these things aside and said some rather hard words:

When that day comes (the judgment day), many will plead with me, "Lord, Lord, have we not prophesied in your name? Have we not exorcised demons by its power? Did we not do many miracles in your name as well?" Then I will declare to them solemnly, "*I never knew you.* Out of my sight, you evildoers!"

Matthew 7:22-23

We must know Jesus and the Father. There's no alternative. And only a personal relationship can bring that about.

GROWING SELF-AWARENESS

This world is constantly lying to you. It's telling you that you're someone you're not. It's saying that you're ordinary. You live at such and such a place and you do this thing or that thing. If you're a Christian you can't go on listening to those lies. You *are* special, very special. You're a son or daughter of God the Father, a brother or sister to Jesus Christ, the King of Kings and Lord of Lords. That fact should influence everything you do and every thought you think. You need to grow in awareness of your dignity. Fr. Brennan Manning, in his book *The Gentle Revolutionaries,* tells how Jesus continually grew in self-awareness of his relationship:

"Son, servant, and beloved of God."

Your quest for a personal relationship with the Father, through Jesus and by the Holy Spirit will require that you continually grow in that very *same* self-awareness. You are "Son (daughter), servant and beloved of God your Father." The remaining chapters of this book deal with the practical "how to do it" steps of entering into this personal relationship. But to close this chapter I'd like to give you a feel for what such a relationship can mean to your own self-awareness. The following description by Fr. Manning of his relationship with the Father is one of the most colorful and fascinating I've ever encountered. It's a lengthy quote, but you'll be richly rewarded by its message.

My foremost reason for wanting to go on is to live more faithfully to my self-awareness, play the role assigned me, and fulfill the destiny appointed me.

That awareness, as I understand it this moment, is to be son of the Father of Jesus, to surrender more fully to the sway of the Holy Spirit. What does it mean to me to live in the continual self-awareness of being son of the Father? The answer is embodied in Jesus, a man like me in all things but ungratefulness, the first-born of many sons, and the image of the invisible God.

To be a son of the Father, like Jesus, is really to delight in this relationship and to fully embrace this identity. It is to enjoy thoroughly and take great pride in finding myself so situated. It is to sense the extraordinary privilege that is mine through no merit of my own. It is to appreciate in a very human sense the dignity of the title bestowed on me and to walk with my head held high. It is to realistically consider myself more fortunate, more endowed and more durable than the president of the

United States, John Paul Getty or anyone possessing the power and wealth to acquire anything he wanted. It is to have the aristocratic bearing of one born to royalty. It is to envy no man anything, for my privileged position transcends all comparisons, eclipses all worldly honors and titles and fills my cup with a joy beyond all telling.

I am son of my Father. Wow!

This is the precious pearl hidden at the deepest layer of my identity, and the living awareness of it is of such personal value to me that fame, success and human recognition are cheap, painted fragments of glass. I feel like the Aga Khan waiting to be weighed, serenely aware of my wealth and rich beyond definition or description.

Do you know who my Father is? He can not only beat up your Father but He holds him protectively in the palm of His hand. He has the wisdom to sketch the plan of this planet in a spare moment (as though jotting down a note to Himself) and the power to breathe life into sperm-ovum, dry bread and the dead. My Father determines the length of your days and tells the sun when to get up in the morning. It will interest you to know that Mont Blanc, the Grand Canyon, the Hope diamond and a black velvet sky glittering with stars are only rude markings of his handsome profile.

Do you know that my Father waits for me each day? That He longs to hear my voice and spend hours alone with me? That He not only knows my name but calls me His little one and

His beloved? Are you aware of how much my Father cares for me, how concerned He is about my movements, how interested He is in the little story of my daily doings? This may blow your mind but my Father, who made the Pleiades and the Orion, makes Himself unconditionally available to me and cancels all His appointments whenever I arrive unannounced.

What is my Father like? One day He grew so apprehensive that I might fail to understand how loving and wise, gentle and powerful He is, that He sent me a complete and perfect expression of Himself in His Son Jesus. Everything my Father has, He entrusted to Jesus so that in looking at Jesus, I can see and know my Father. Of course Jesus has a different personality so that He can be Himself but He is essentially the same. All the same attitudes and characteristics just signed with His own signature. Let me tell you the most beautiful and thrilling thing He ever said to me. I wake up to it each morning and lay there sleepy, dazed and happy because I always hear it as for the first time. ''As the Father has loved me, so do I love you.''

I will listen patiently and with interest to the story of your hard-earned successes, your brilliant victories and myriad acquisitions. I will rejoice when you tell me how many friends you have and how happy you are, but don't ever feel sorry for me. When you hear how gifted I am, you will say to your best friend, ''Of all the men I have ever known, Brennan

107

is the one I envy most.''

The Gentle Revolutionaries, pp. 99-102.

CHAPTER 5

Can a Catholic Be "Saved"?

As the meeting broke up teenagers were quickly exiting the gym. I had just finished speaking to a parish confirmation class and was waiting to answer any questions when a girl in her mid-teens came up and introduced herself:

"Hi, I'm Sharon Smith — my father works with you."

We exchanged the normal small talk for a minute, then to my surprise she announced:

"You know, I was 'saved' last summer at an evangelical meeting over in Manchester."

I smiled my approval, but couldn't help wondering, "Was she really saved then — or did she simply come to *know it* for the first time?" You see, that word "saved" normally isn't used by Catholics, so there's much confusion about it.

Of course our evangelical Protestant brothers aren't confused about that word. They know exactly what it means. And they have a knack for asking Catholics some rather embarrassing questions, such as:

"Have you been saved? Are you a born-again Christian? Have you got the Baptism of the Holy

Spirit?''

Now we Catholics aren't embarrassed because of our beliefs, but because we simply don't know how to answer those questions. Let's face it, we just don't talk that way. And try to explain your infant baptism to an evangelical brother:

''Ah-hah,'' exclaims our friend, ''you're not really a Christian then. You have to be immersed to be baptized properly — then you've got to be born again.''

When it comes to salvation, the most important topic you and I will ever consider, we're usually at a loss for words. Perhaps the problem is that our wealth of Catholic theology has never been boiled down to easily understood principles similar to those our Protestant brothers use. I think it should be; so in these next pages I'll attempt to put our Catholic views of salvation into a form you can grasp easily. It's important that you're sure of your salvation, because knowing you *are* saved is essential for a personal relationship with God.

IDEAS IN COMMON

First let's explore some things we have in common with our Protestant brothers. Essentially all Christian churches teach the basic truths of salvation in much the same manner. It's in the process of ''Christian Initiation'' that you'll see differences. Now Christian initiation is simply the process by which a particular church makes non-Christians into Christians. It usually means that they also become members of that particular church. But the apparent differences in this initiation process are essentially differences in *terminology* and ritual, rather than theology. So we find

110

that behind all these words and ceremonies there is much we agree on.

Christianity, then, regardless of the brand, teaches that God has intervened in our affairs to "save" us from the consequence of sin which is eternal death (or hell). Christianity says that God doesn't come only to mankind in general, but to each and every individual. Every one of us at one time or another will feel the call of God. Scripture states:

> . . . for he (God) wants *all men* to be saved and come to know the truth.
>
> *1 Timothy 2:4*

This divine invitation, however, sometimes finds us unreceptive. Cardinal Suenens writes:

> We have an instinctive fear of God intruding into our affairs, even if they are going badly. We stiffen in the face of any interference from outside; we regard it as estrangement, and we fear a wisdom that does not obey our laws. The very idea of intervention on the part of God makes us uneasy. We usually steer clear of those passages in the Bible which do not conform to our categories. God's nearness disturbs us. We take exception whenever his action gets too close and upsets our daily routine. Our real fear, however, ought to be that we may not recognize God's coming in time, that we may not be there when he knocks at our door.
>
> *A New Pentecost?*, pp. 90-91.

Christianity also teaches that God took the initiative in this salvation process. His first step was to form a ''people,'' Israel, to whom he revealed his will. Second, and most important, he sent his only begotten Son, Jesus Christ, to be the means of acquiring his forgiveness and salvation. Saint Paul writes:

> God has not destined us for wrath but for acquiring salvation *through our Lord Jesus Christ.*
>
> *1 Thessalonians 5:9*

The whole aim of Jesus' Gospel was salvation. Scripture describes his message as the ''word of salvation,'' the ''way of salvation'' and the ''power of salvation.'' His message was always one of hope:

> . . . for I did not come to condemn the world but to *save* it.
>
> *John 12:47*

Jesus passed on to his disciples and to *all* his followers to come that same mission of bringing the message of salvation to the world.

> Go into the whole world and proclaim the good news to all creation. The man who believes in it and accepts baptism will be *saved;* the man who refuses to believe in it will be condemned.
>
> *Mark 16:15-16*

Christianity goes on to teach that this ''good news'' of salvation was not directed at people who were already ''good,'' but to sinners.

112

You can depend on this as worthy of full acceptance: that Christ Jesus came into the world to *save sinners.*

1 Timothy 1:15

Jesus said it this way:

I have not come to invite the self-righteous to a change of heart, but *sinners.*

Luke 5:32

Yes, the Father put no conditions of "goodness" on his salvation. He made it absolutely free. No one would earn it by good deeds.

The Christian Churches explain further that Jesus revealed exactly what God was like: a Father whose hallmarks were mercy and forgiveness. So great was his merciful love that, through Jesus, he paid what *we owed* because of our sinfulness. The U.S. Bishops tell us:

Instruction must remind the student of the sufferings and the death on the cross which Christ endured to *destroy the effects of sin.*

But it must go on to speak eloquently of God's forgiveness. Even though a man sins, he can be pardoned. The power of grace is greater than that of sin. The superabundant love of God restores the penitent and *draws him toward salvation.*

Basic Teachings for Catholic Religious Education, #16.

So all Christian Churches teach that you are "saved" by God's love. You cannot know that you are saved unless you first know the love of Jesus and the Father for you *personally.* God is love, Jesus is the personification of his love, and Jesus on the cross is the visible sign of just how deep his love is. The Father wants you to know that you're saved; he wants you to know that you're loved; he wants you to look at Jesus hanging on the cross and begin, just begin, to understand what his love is really all about. God is a Father who will stop at nothing to prove his love for you: this is the universal Christian message.

PROTESTANT INITIATION

Every Christian Church must take these general ideas about salvation and translate them into meaningful salvation events called *Christian initiation.* And since we're trying to get a clear, fresh view of salvation, it would be good to explore the way in which our Protestant brothers view Christian initiation. Not only will this help our own understanding, it will also help that communications problem we spoke of earlier.

Of course there are as many different initiation processes as there are Christian Churches — literally hundreds. So again we'll have to take a general approach. But by paying particular attention to Evangelical Protestants (those who claim a ''born-again'' experience), we'll get a good overview. You see, evangelicals form about half of all Protestants and are one of the few Christian groups that are growing significantly today. Some estimates put their number at 50 million adult Americans.

Now the first principle of Protestantism which affects salvation is the belief that the Bible is the *sole* authority upon which any doctrine is based. Our Catholic concept, which says that Tradition can be used to interpret Scripture, is ruled out. This sometimes leads to a second principle called "literal interpretation" which is particularly strong among Evangelical Protestants. Therefore, if you want to understand Christian initiation in a Protestant framework, you must go to the Bible and see what it has to say.

Let's begin with an incident described in the Acts of the Apostles. Paul and his companion Silas confront the jailer who has been shaken by an earthquake and the obvious power of God, and who now seeks to know this God. The jailer asks:

> "Men, what must I do to be saved?" Their answer was, "Believe in the Lord Jesus and you will be saved, and all your household."
>
> *Acts 16:30-31*

So the first step is to *believe.* Our Protestant brothers will be quick to point out, and quite correctly, that belief means more than merely believing there was such a person as Jesus Christ. To believe *in* Jesus means to acknowledge that he is the Son of God the Father, that he is Lord, that he died and rose again to defeat sin and death, and that through him your sins are forgiven. In short, belief as St. Paul speaks of it demands more than your intellectual recognition of a person called Jesus Christ; it asks that you make him *Lord* of your life, that you live by the truths he taught. Up to this point Catholics have no argument with Protestants whatsoever.

The second step also has some common ground with Catholic teaching. Saint Paul writes:

> For if you confess with your lips that Jesus is Lord, and believe in your heart that God raised him from the dead, you will be saved. Faith in

the heart leads to justification, confession on the lips to salvation.

Romans 10:9-10

Speaking out what you truly believe in your heart is "confession on the lips." A person is asked to confess that he's a sinner, that he repents of his sinfulness, and that he makes Jesus Christ the Lord of his life — his only Savior.

Catholic and Protestant teaching begin to depart from one another on this second point when Protestants (particularly Evangelicals) claim that you must confess Jesus by *name*. The name "Jesus" must be spoken or acknowledged before you're saved. They cite two scriptures to support this argument. The first was spoken by St. Peter as he addressed the Jewish Sanhedrin (the supreme court of Jerusalem):

There is no salvation in anyone else, for there is no other name in the whole world given to men by which we are to be saved.

Acts 4:12

This scripture is backed up with the words of Jesus from St. John's Gospel:

I am the way, and the truth, and the life; no one *comes to the Father* but through me.

John 14:6

This term "comes to the Father" is taken to mean only salvation. But in the previous chapters we've seen that Jesus was actually talking about *how* we come into a personal relationship with the Father. In that case Jesus certainly is the only way. It's also true

116

that only through Jesus' sacrifice on the cross can anyone achieve salvation. However, Evangelical Protestants demand, based on these scriptures, that the word "Jesus" actually be spoken by the person seeking salvation. As we shall see, Catholic thinking is somewhat different.

Another distinction between Evangelical Protestants and Catholics is the evangelical emphasis on a "born-again" experience. This term "born-again" comes from the King James Version (KJV) of Jesus' talk with Nicodemus, a high Jewish official of his day. The scripture reads:

There was a man of the Pharisees, named Nicodemus, a ruler of the Jews: The same came to Jesus by night, and said unto him, Rabbi, we know that thou art a teacher come from God: for no man can do these miracles that thou doest, except God be with him. Jesus answered and said unto him, Verily, verily, I say unto thee, Except a man be *born again,* he cannot see the kingdom of God. Nicodemus saith unto him, How can a man be born when he is old? Can he enter the second time into his mother's womb, and be born? Jesus answered, Verily, verily, I say unto thee, Except a man be born of water and of the Spirit, he cannot enter into the kingdom of God. That which is born of the flesh is flesh; and that which is born of the Spirit is spirit. Marvel not that I said unto thee, *Ye must be born again.*

John 3:1-7 (KJV)

Now both Catholics and Protestants agree with this literal translation. In stating that you must be "born-again," Jesus is saying that any man-made, preconceived notions of how the Father wants to relate to us must die. Rebirth in water and the Spirit means a rebirth of our spiritual existence. Rebirth is transformation. Rebirth is renewal. Rebirth is the Father's life coming into us and starting to grow. Rebirth is an interior revolution. That is why Saint Paul triumphantly declares:

> . . . if anyone is in Christ, he is a *new creation.*
>
> 2 Corinthians 5:17

Because this change is so radical, an adult who's "born again" actually *experiences* that divine injection of new life. There's no way to describe it except as a religious experience of the Father's life and love pouring into a person's soul. So an adult who becomes Christian should expect this infusing of new life to be quite profound.

When you introduce the idea of religious experience, however, you should watch out for a "legalism of experience" to creep in. By this I mean that you may begin to expect that because most people react a certain way, everyone should react the same way. If they don't, they're obviously not "born again." Now that simply isn't true. You see, it automatically excludes people who might respond to the Father differently, yet just as sincerely. So making salvation depend upon a specific religious experience is deadly wrong. (Actually, very few established Protestant Churches would require a specific religious experience as evidence of salvation even if they do profess the necessity of being "born again.") In short, you can say that being "born again" is a valid religious experience, but you must be open to the possibility of its happening differently in different people.

Taking a broad view, therefore, you can identify the following essential parts of Protestant Christian initiation:

1. You must believe and accept all that Jesus taught.
2. You must profess your faith in these beliefs.
3. You must depart from past sinful ways by receiving the Father's new life which makes you a "born-again Christian."

Following these steps doesn't necessarily mean that the new Christian belongs to a specific Church or denomination, although it may. Sometimes after receiving salvation a believer is what you might call a "free-lance Christian." As such he might go to various denominational Churches, or perhaps to a gathering of like-minded Christians who are not attached to any denomination. In general, Protestants seem to be much less attached to a specific Church or denomination than are Catholics.

Now a few Protestant denominations believe that they alone are the real Christians. The Catholic Church, however, says that any Church which fulfills the basics of Christian initiation can truly give us salvation. In speaking of these non-Catholic Churches Vatican II said:

> For the Spirit of Christ has not refrained from using them (the non-Catholic Churches) as means of salvation. . . .
>
> *Documents of Vatican II*, Ecumenism, #3.

The techniques they use may seem strange to us Catholics, nevertheless they fulfill the requirements, for Vatican II added that:

> The brethren divided from us also carry out many of the sacred actions of the Christian religion. Undoubtedly, in ways that vary according to the condition of each Church or Community, these actions can truly engender a life of grace, and can be rightly described as capable of providing access to the community of salvation.
>
> *Documents of Vatican II,* Decree on Ecumenism, #3.

One further point about Protestant initiation: many Protestants don't view "being saved" and Baptism as events which are rigidly connected to one another. Sometimes Baptism is separated from the salvation experience by a considerable length of time. In the Catholic Church, of course, the opposite is true.

CATHOLIC INITIATION

Now it might surprise you to learn that these basic principles of Protestant initiation are exactly the same in the Catholic Church. Belief and acceptance of Jesus as Lord, profession of faith and the idea of new, divine life entering and transforming us are all part of Catholic teaching. Vatican II said:

> The mission of the Church concerns the salvation of men, which is to be achieved by *belief* in Christ and by His *grace.*
>
> *Documents of Vatican II,* Decree on the Apostolate of the Laity, #6.

The Catholic Church goes a step beyond Protestantism when it states that Tradition also must be considered if we're to find the correct procedure for Christian initiation.

> Basing itself upon sacred *Scripture and tradition,* it (Vatican II) teaches that the Church . . . is necessary for salvation.
>
> *Documents of Vatican II,* The Church, #14.

Tradition, using Scripture as a basis, has taught the Church that this whole idea of Christian initiation should revolve around Baptism. Catholics have always believed that a person gained salvation through Baptism, and at the same time he was joined to the Church. So in the normal course of events, salvation, Baptism and joining the Church are all lumped together in such a way that it's easy to assume they can't be separated. Catholics hardly ever talk about them being separated. That's why we find Vatican II saying:

> For Christ, made present to us in His Body, which is the Church, is the one Mediator and the unique Way of salvation. In explicit terms He Himself affirmed the necessity of faith and baptism . . . and thereby affirmed also the necessity of the Church, for through baptism as through a door men enter the Church.
>
> *Documents of Vatican II,* The Church, #14.

In its theology, however, the Church has always said that under extraordinary circumstances they can be achieved separately. Yes, you can be saved without being Baptized, or without joining the Church, but it's not the normal course of events, and it's definitely not a safe way to proceed. It's important that you understand what the Church believes: all men are called to salvation *in* Jesus Christ.

> Besides, as the Church has always held and continues to hold, Christ in His boundless love freely underwent His passion and death because of the sins of *all men,* so that *all* might attain salvation.
>
> *Documents of Vatican II,* Declaration on the Relationship of the Church to Non-Christians, #4.

All men are called to salvation, but obviously all men haven't heard the ''Good News'' of the Father's love, forgiveness and new life. What about those people who have never heard the Gospel of Jesus Christ? Our Protestant evangelical friends would say, ''We're sorry, but unless you confess Jesus as Lord and accept him as your savior, there is no salvation.''

The Catholic Church (and some Protestant Churches as well) says, however, that God's mercy is so great that any man who truly seeks to live a good life and find God, can possibly achieve salvation without directly hearing the message of Jesus. The odds are against this happening, yet it's possible. The Church Fathers said:

> Those also can attain to everlasting salvation who through no fault of their own do not know the gospel of Christ or His Church, yet *sincerely* seek God and, moved by grace, strive by their deeds to do His will as it is known to them through the dictates of conscience. Nor does divine Providence deny the help neces-

sary for salvation to those who, without blame on their part, have not yet arrived at an explicit knowledge of God, but who strive to live a good life, thanks to His grace.

Documents of Vatican II, The Church, #16.

The Church is saying that in their own way these people have ''effectively accepted Jesus Christ'' even though they may never have heard his name. Therefore, Catholics break down salvation into three categories:

1. Non-Judaeo-Christian Peoples

These people have never received God's direct revelation. Saint Paul says that they will be judged by how well they keep the law which they have in their own hearts:

When Gentiles who do not have the law keep it as by instinct, these men although without the law serve as a law for themselves. They show that the demands of the law are written in their hearts. Their conscience bears witness together with that law, and their thoughts will accuse or defend them on the day when, in accordance with the gospel I preach, God will pass judgment on the secrets of men through Christ Jesus.

Romans 2:14-16

Let's face it, these people have a tough road to travel. Without any direct revelation of the Father's will, many a diversion lies in their path such as false religions, materialism, lust and the powers of evil.

123

Anyone who's counted in this category is on an extremely difficult and dangerous path to salvation.

2. The Jewish People

These people were chosen by the Father to receive his direct revelation, yet for one reason or another they have not heard the message of the Messiah, Jesus Christ. Now St. Paul called the Jewish Law "a clear pattern of knowledge and truth" *(Romans 2:20)*, but he forcefully pointed out that salvation was obtained through the Father's mercy and Jesus' sacrifice — not from the Law. So those who lived by the Law would be judged by it. In this category we should expect the percentage of those achieving salvation to be higher because they have had the Law as a guide. Still the task is very difficult.

3. Christians

The Catholic Church says that " . . . all men are called to salvation by the grace of God" (Documents of Vatican II, The Church, #13), yet Christians, and only Christians, are completely equipped and empowered to gain salvation. They *are* special. Christians have entered a unique relationship with the Father of the universe; they are truly sons of God. Yet this tremendous salvation is not the result of anything they've done; as valuable as it is, they've obtained it free of charge. All they've done is become a follower of Jesus. The Church Fathers said:

> The followers of Christ are called by God, not according to their accomplishments, but according to His own purpose and grace. They

are justified in the Lord Jesus, and through baptism sought in faith they *truly become sons of God and sharers in the divine nature.*

Documents of Vatican II, The Church, #40.

Yes, a Christian is truly unique in God's creation. And if a Christian fails to understand just how unique he really is, he has missed the main point of Jesus' message. You see, a Christian is more than just saved in the sense that most people think of salvation. The Christian has humbled himself enough to accept Jesus Christ as his Lord; therefore the Father has exalted him to *full* sonship.

While we're comparing Catholic and Protestant initiation, it would be good to mention one other point. An Evangelical Protestant will ask, ''Have you been saved?'' This question implies that being saved is a one-time event. Some even say, ''Once saved, always saved.'' The Catholic point of view is somewhat different. While the Catholic Church views Baptism as the ''salvation event,'' it considers this a starting point in a *process* of salvation. In other words, salvation is looked upon as a life-long walk during which we grow in our relationship with the Father. Our salvation begins at the moment we're saved, but it doesn't end until we're united with the Father as Jesus is. Thus John McKenzie, S.J., the noted Scripture scholar, writes:

The reception of salvation by the saved is conceived as a process rather than a single act. . . . One of the recurring heresies of the history of Christianity has been the belief that salvation could be finally and completely achieved by a single act, whether that act be conceived as the predestination of God, the saving death of Jesus Christ, or the reception of faith and baptism.

Dictionary of the Bible, pp. 762-763.

Because of this view, Catholics normally don't talk about "being saved" as a particular event. However, a Catholic should know that he is "saved" and that the "salvation process" will bring him more and more into union with the Father. He can, of course, turn away from the Father's call after starting the salvation process and be lost once again. We Catholics call this *mortal sin.* But if there's no mortal sin present, then the Catholic Christian has the right and the duty to say: "Yes, I am saved."

BRETHREN, WHAT MUST WE DO?

You should now be at the same point that many faithful Jews found themselves at on Pentecost. They heard the mighty noise of the Holy Spirit come upon the Apostles; they heard them speak out boldly in many tongues; they heard Peter proclaim the Gospel. Then, moved by these events into belief in Jesus' salvation, they wanted it for themselves. So they asked, "Brethren, what must we do?"

In the pages ahead I'll explain exactly what you must do to be sure of your salvation — to come into a personal relationship with the Father. It would be easy to simply list numerous steps to follow and prayers to recite, but I want to be truthful with you. It may or may not be that simple. Some people will enter a personal relationship by the time they finish this chapter. Others will need a bit more time. Nevertheless, this relationship is available to anyone who truly seeks it.

Before going through a step-by-step method of making the correct response, you need to examine what has happened (or should have happened) in your own Catholic Christian initiation up to this point. You see, our sacramental system has much beauty and power; it was definitely begun by Jesus himself. But it has undergone a steady evolution since then. In that evolution things have been added which sometimes make the purpose of the sacraments unclear. Also, people have often looked at the ceremony or ritual by itself, ignoring the real meaning behind it (even when that meaning was announced). Therefore, Vatican II admitted:

> With the passage of time . . . there have crept into the rites of the sacraments and sacramentals certain features which have rendered their nature and purpose less clear to the people of today.
>
> *Documents of Vatican II,* Constitution on the Sacred Liturgy, #62.

Since Vatican II, we Catholics have seen many changes take place in the sacraments, all directed toward making their real meaning stand out. So let's take a look at our modern sacramental initiation.

BAPTISM

Peter the Apostle wrote:

> *You are now saved* by a baptismal bath which corresponds to this exactly. This baptism is no removal of physical stain, but the pledge *to*

God of an irreproachable conscience through
the resurrection of Jesus Christ.

1 Peter 3:21

Notice how he stresses that we have something to give
"to God" as part of Baptism. What we give is our free
will. So let's list the key things that must take place
through our free will during Baptism. Remember
we're not talking about the external things that must
happen (i.e. the ceremony), but rather about a person's
inner response. There are basically three inner actions:

1. REPENTANCE

The first recorded words of Jesus in the New Testament as he began his public ministry are: "Repent,
for the kingdom of heaven is close at hand" *(Matthew
4:17 JB)*. Repentance is a major theme in the New
Testament. Jesus (and the Apostles after him) constantly preached it. As I said before, it's surprising
that most Christians really don't understand repentance. Too many people think it means simply feeling
sorry for their sins. Others say it means making a vow
not to "do it" again, or perhaps the act of going to
confession itself. Now all these may be part of repentance, but they're not what repentance really is. The
word which we translate "repent" literally means "to
turn away from." In other words, to do an about-face,
to turn in an entirely different direction. It's a radical
change; not simply a confession that "I'll try harder
next time, Father." Baptism marks our turning onto a
new road: the road leading into the Father's kingdom.
It is truly a change of lifestyle and a change of heart.

2. COMMITMENT

The kind of repentance we've been talking about demands *firm* commitment. Essentially we're reshaping our whole life — our whole inner selves. We're making a free decision to turn to Jesus Christ and make him the standard by which we judge things, turning our backs on worldly standards. Cardinal Suenens has written:

> To become truly a Christian one must agree, in full freedom, to be converted, to repent and turn to Christ, and accept his Holy Spirit. We cannot escape these obligations.
>
> *A New Pentecost?*, pp. 131-132.

But Cardinal Suenens isn't introducing something new. St. Leo the Great said essentially the same thing over 1500 years ago:

> But it is only when we believe and *commit* ourselves fully to the lordship of Jesus that we begin to enter into the fullness of understanding that he promised.
>
> Anne Field, O.S.B., *The Binding of the Strong Man*, pp. 75-76.

Without true commitment, Christianity will be an empty, powerless, moral exercise. Genuine commitment to the Lordship of Jesus brings life, joy, peace and power. Then, and only then, does Christianity become meaningful. Remember, this commitment must *not* be made to a set of religious rules and doctrines, but rather to the person of Jesus Christ himself. Religious rules, doctrines, Church structures, etc. are all essential for Christianity to work well, but your commitment is not to those things. Your commitment must be to the Lordship of Jesus Christ. Commitment to the Church, etc., will naturally follow from that.

3. CONFESSION OF THE LIPS

As I said previously, the person being baptized is expected to confess openly with his lips that he has repented and committed his life to Jesus Christ. But in saying so, he must be confessing true repentance and true commitment. The words must indicate that something has happened inside. A verbal confession without this interior change is meaningless; it carries no assurance of salvation.

Now it should be obvious that an infant cannot be expected to repent. He actually has nothing to repent of. Baptism in this case can rid the child of what we Catholics call "original sin" but it's only the first step in the process called "Christian initiation." The Church knew this when it began baptizing infants, so the commitment portion of baptism evolved into another rite or sacrament called Confirmation.

CONFIRMATION

Most people are really confused about the purpose of Confirmation. Its basic purpose is to *complete* your Christian initiation and to empower you. For those of us baptized as infants, an "adult commitment" was missing. Confirmation is where we pledge our commitment to the Christian life. And this idea of commitment is so important that Vatican II emphasized it by saying:

The rite of confirmation is to be revised and the *intimate connection* which this sacrament has with the whole of Christian initiation is to be more lucidly set forth; for this reason it will be fitting for candidates to renew their baptismal promises just before they are confirmed.

Documents of Vatican II, Constitution on the
Sacred Liturgy, #71.

Now some people will tell you that the main purpose of Confirmation is to give the Holy Spirit. The Spirit then enables you to become a committed Christian. These people have the cart before the horse. The Holy Spirit does indeed give power to live the Christian life (perhaps more than you imagine), and the Spirit is given in both Baptism and Confirmation to accomplish this. But if you want to receive this complete empowering of the Spirit, you'll first have to make a sincere and total commitment. After that commitment, you'll receive the Spirit's power to live up to those promises.

Unfortunately, for many of us our Baptism and early Christian education were largely a matter of parental coercion, however well-intentioned. We "inherited Christianity," so to speak. However, as some people have said, "God doesn't have any grandchildren, only children." In other words, the only way we can become a full-fledged child of the Father is to make our *own* commitment — a personal decision as a mature person to follow Jesus Christ. Cardinal Suenens wrote:

Christianity which we have inherited, which has its foundation mainly in the family and education, must mature into a Christianity of choice, based on a *personal decision* and embraced with full consciousness.

A New Pentecost?, p. 125.

It's sad, but true, that a person can grow up in the Catholic Church — be baptized, confirmed, receive any other sacrament for which he's eligible — and still never make a *real* commitment to Jesus Christ. His whole life in the Church can be based on external rules and rituals while his heart remains untouched by what Jesus teaches and his values remain fixed on the material world. Yes, the Church offers us salvation through the sacraments, but they're "sacraments of faith" and they make demands on us, demands of repentance, commitment and confession. Again let me emphasize that this is nothing new — it's not Vatican II theology. It's *basic* Christianity. Saint Leo the Great said:

But unless a man believes in Jesus Christ, true God and true man, and accepts him as *his own* Savior, the salvation that is offered to the whole of mankind will be of no avail to him.

Anne Field, O.S.B., *The Binding of the Strong Man,* p. 85.

In his book *A New Pentecost?* Cardinal Suenens suggests this definition:

A Christian is a changed person, a convert: he has turned away from himself, so as to adhere to Jesus of Nazareth who, for his sake, died and rose from the dead. He has made a *personal discovery of Jesus,* and acknowledged him as the Christ, the unique Son of the Father, the anointed One of the Holy Spirit. He has found in Jesus the Savior and Lord of all mankind. At the heart of every true surrender to Christ one finds, in one form or another, an echo of Claudel's cry on the evening of his conversion, when he suddenly saw Jesus with new eyes: "Now, all of a sudden, you are Someone!"

A New Pentecost?, pp. 117-118.

A Christian doesn't merely receive various sacraments, go to Church on Sunday and follow the Church's external laws. Christianity is an *interior revolution* leading to a personal relationship with the Father through Jesus and nothing less. Father Brennan Manning suggests:

This and this alone is authentic Christianity. Not a code of do's and don'ts, not a tedious moralizing, not a list of forbidding commandments, and certainly not the necessary minimum requirement for avoiding the pains of hell. Life in the Spirit is the thrill and the excitement of falling in love with Jesus Christ.

The Gentle Revolutionaries, p. 131.

Therefore our Confirmation should have been the end of a well-rounded Christian initiation process, emphasizing an adult type commitment to the Lordship of Jesus. If it wasn't, some essential points may have been left out. One reason for the weakness we see in Catholic Christians today is a lack of *real* commitment which should have been made at this pivotal point in our Christian life — Confirmation. We'll look into remaking that essential commitment shortly, but first we need to clear up two other serious problems. These can interfere with our ability to make that renewed commitment.

LEGALISM

A good Mohammedan is never without his prayer mat, for he must pray a certain number of times each day, no matter where he is or what he's doing. There's an old story about a Mohammedan pursuing a man he intended to murder. Upon hearing the call to pray, this Mohammedan stopped his pursuit, took out his prayer mat, and hurriedly said his prayer. Finished, he continued to seek his victim.

This man fulfilled the legal requirements of his church's ritual, but his heart wasn't in their message — he was content only to follow rules. That's *legalism*, an insidious infection that affects us all.

Saint Paul had been a Pharisee, so he understood legalism. He knew it all too often breeds a piety centered on ''doing things'' — the heart isn't really transformed; the depths of a man's being remain unchanged. Paul lashed out against this legalism constantly, especially in his epistles to the Romans and Galatians. The futility of religious legalism was one of his pet themes. To the Colossians he wrote:

> . . . why should you be bound by rules that say, ''Do not handle! Do not taste! Do not touch!'' as though you were still living a life bounded by this world? Such prescriptions deal with things that perish in their use. They are based on merely human precepts and doctrines. While these make a certain show of

wisdom in their affected piety, humility, and bodily austerity, their chief effect is that they indulge men's pride.

Colossians 2:20-23

Too many people, even today, see doctrines as magic formulas written by holy men who received them directly from God. Doctrines are, in fact, based upon the experiences of people who sought out a relationship with God successfully and have tried to show us the same path. C.S. Lewis once wrote:

Doctrines are not God: they are only a kind of map. But that map is based on the experience of hundreds of people who really were in touch with God. . . .

Mere Christianity, p. 136.

Now religious legalism is a pitfall we all stumble into at one time or another. It's so easy to substitute a rule for the self-sacrificing love Jesus calls us to. The words he spoke to men practicing religious legalism in his day were included in Sacred Scripture for our benefit. We can't limit their application to people living long ago in another religious culture. Jesus says to *us:*

Thus you present to view a holy exterior while hypocrisy and evil fill you within.

Matthew 23:28

According to Jesus, merely following rules and doctrines is not enough. It may be necessary but it's not sufficient. The stuff of a person's heart is what really counts. If our hearts are turned to God, the rules and doctrines will be of some use to us. But if our hearts aren't turned, no matter how carefully we follow the rules, we miss his call. The Father gave us rules, commandments and religious doctrines, not as a means to salvation, but as guides or signposts. Of course all the signposts in the world won't get us to our destination if we refuse to move our hearts toward the Father.

This idea of "following rules" leads to another problem: believing that Church membership alone can buy us salvation. It can't. And those who think it can are greatly deceived. People in this category are always looking for that minimum requirement to "just get by." In short, their body goes to church, but not their heart. Vatican II spoke out strongly when it said:

> He is *not saved,* however, who, though he is part of the body of the Church, does not persevere in charity (i.e. Christian love). He remains indeed in the bosom of the Church, but, as it were, only in a "bodily" manner and not "in his heart."
>
> *Documents of Vatican II,* The Church, #14.

Let's face it, we all "take our bodies to Church" sometimes while our hearts remain elsewhere. We're not talking about that. We're talking about people who habitually go to church each Sunday only to satisfy the Church's law. Vatican II is saying that simply hauling your body to church isn't fulfilling that law. Your heart must come along also.

This modern legalism breeds a negative approach to Christianity. Father Brennan Manning writes about a survey given to graduating seniors at a small, Catholic liberal arts college in the midwest. Asked what being a Christian means, their answers were so much alike they were condensed into a single paragraph:

> To be a Christian means that I must go to Mass on Sundays and holydays, abstain from meat on Ash Wednesday and Good Friday; I cannot practice birth control, get a divorce, procure an abortion or see an X-rated movie. There are no escapes from the rigors of my Catholic existence.
>
> *Prophets and Lovers*, p. 43.

My own experience while visiting parishes throughout the country tells me the survey would yield similar answers no matter where the questions were asked. I can imagine the Apostle Paul returning today, hearing these replies, shaking his head and beginning to weep. It's sad indeed that so many Christians have missed the whole point of Christianity. They seek their salvation by following negative rules rather than by following the positive God-man, Jesus, who constantly put rules aside. His message was always the same: "Come to *me*, believe in *me*, learn to love by loving like I love, seek *me*, know *me*!" Saint Paul adds:

> . . . a man is not justified by legal observance but *by faith in Jesus Christ.*
>
> *Galatians 2:16*

So the answer to our legalistic problem is faith — faith in Jesus, not faith in rules. But exactly what is *faith?* Well, the faith Paul speaks of isn't merely "belief." Many people believe Jesus Christ existed, but they really don't have faith in him. Faith moves beyond belief. It makes a person's inner-self actually come into contact with the divine life offered by the Father. When we react to this encounter, we can believe with both our head and our heart. In other words, faith involves not only a person's head knowledge of Jesus, but his heart knowledge as well. Cardinal Suenens writes:

> . . . let us rid ourselves immediately of any misunderstanding. We *must not forget* that faith is basically an adherence, not to a set of propositions, but to God who reveals himself to us. Faith is a living encounter with a living God; it is formulated in the Church within the context of experience. Doctrine is the expression or common definition of the experience of God, as lived by the apostles and the Christian community and then passed on to us.
>
> *A New Pentecost?*, p. 56.

To merely follow the rules will result in a dull and lifeless Christianity. We must understand that, first and foremost, Christianity is a love affair: a passionate love, an ''on fire'' love, an irrational-at-times love, a forgiving love, and most important, a sincere from-the-heart love. If that sort of love isn't there first, legal observances (even in God's name) will gain us nothing. Father Brennan Manning has said:

> Christianity is not a system of laws, an ethical code, a philosophy, *but a love*.
>
> *Prophets and Lovers*, p. 48.

LEGALISM OF PURGATORY

Now there's another fatal trap we Catholics can easily fall into; it's called, "Purgatory — A Second Chance." I once heard a fine Catholic woman say, "If the Catholic Church stops believing in purgatory, I'm gonna find a Church that does. That's the only way I'll ever make it."

Now this seems to be a popular idea. It says in effect that the Father is a God who's going to make us "pay up" for all those rotten things we've done. Only after we've paid the price will we be allowed into heaven. When we think this way we fail to see the all loving Father who Jesus revealed. When we think this way we miss the whole point of the prodigal son parable where our Father waits with forgiving love instead of punishment. We don't hear Jesus saying, "Come to me and know that you're forgiven." You see, it's inconceivable that a Father who would call us to a personal relationship would then turn around and say, "See here now, you've committed XXXX number of sins in your lifetime — now I'm going to make you pay for them." No, the Father is beyond such pettiness. Furthermore, Sacred Scripture indicates that there's really only one punishment for sin — and that's death. So the New Testament message, the "Good News," is that we're off the hook. Jesus paid that awful price on the cross — our punishment was laid upon him. Well then, what's purgatory all about if it isn't payment for sin?

First, let's rid ourselves of the idea that purgatory has to be a "place"; the Church never has defined exactly what purgatory is. I must personally agree with theologians who consider it a "process" — a kind of finishing school for the soul. You see, in speaking about heaven the Scriptures note that . . .

. . . nothing profane shall enter it.

Revelation 21:27

So when these bodies we now live in die, we'll have souls in various states of holiness. Some souls among us will be very close to the Father. They are the "Saints" who need little or no transformation before becoming "one with him." Others of us will have a long way to go before we're ready to stand in the Father's perfect love. We'll have to undergo a process of "Transformation" and that transforming process is what we call "purgatory." Anthony Wilhelm has written:

> Purgatory has been described as a "place" where we would go for a certain "time" to be purified by "fire." We must not misunderstand this — purgatory is certainly not hell for a short time, nor a vast torture chamber where God revenges himself upon trapped souls nor is there time in our sense in this purgatory state. These metaphors attempt to describe the paradox of purgatory — a state of joy and yet of suffering.

> In this purgation what we are doing is growing in love, by submitting ourselves to the burning, penetrating, purifying power of God's love. We realize clearly our immature self-love, our ingratitude, sloth, and attachments to sin. We "grow up" in love, break away from our childish self-centeredness. Our real self then emerges, perfected, totally absorbed in God, totally in love.

Christ Among Us, pp. 419-420.

I've devised an illustration which helps me grasp what this process is all about — how sin, salvation and purgatory work. In this illustration there are three "places" — the World, Heaven and Hell. There are also two roads — one leads to Heaven (the narrow one), and one leads to Hell (the wide one). There's another important feature — a bridge called salvation. Now at some point on the wide road leading to darkness (hell) we find "the salvation bridge." This bridge, supported by Jesus, allows us to cross to the narrow road leading to Heaven. As we cross, the Father's divine life enters and the transforming process begins. The end result of this transformation is our total union with the Father (or Heaven).

Now beginning at the bridge, we find that whenever we grow in the Father's love and in our personal relationship with him, we'll move "up" the narrow

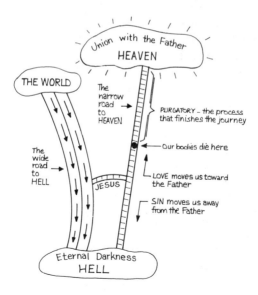

road. However, when we let sin enter our lives, we fall back down the road toward darkness. So yielding to the Father is a step toward union with him, while sin is a step backward — away from him. Notice that the path stretches all the way from Hell to Heaven indicating that a person can get on the right path just before entering Hell, or God forbid, a person can move all the way down the narrow road because of mortal sin and be lost forever. Most Christians, however, will find themselves beginning about halfway along the road and their life here on earth will bring about slow but steady progress toward the Father. Sin may now and then make them lose a few steps, but all in all, they make progress. Obviously, some make more progress than others and upon the body's death some souls will have only a short distance to go while others will have a great deal of road ahead. Purgatory, then, is the process which completes the ''walk to the Father.'' It's not a second chance nor is it a process easier than the transforming process we are now in. Most theologians agree that it's far worse. In any event, we should make as much progress as possible toward the Father *now*, not later. Putting off progress until later is essentially walking in the wrong direction. St. Paul said:

> Now is the acceptable time! Now is the day of salvation!
>
> *2 Corinthians 6:2*

I've tried to show you in this section how religious legalism can very easily breed death, not life. If you're trusting in your faithful observance of religious rules as your means of salvation, you're standing on shaky ground. If you're waiting for purgatory to start your walk to the Father, you're greatly deceived. Salvation comes when you have a living faith in a living God who you know through a personal relationship. You shouldn't try it any other way.

STEPS TO KNOWING

We've looked at the basics of salvation, seen how different churches translate those basics into Christian initiation, looked at our own Catholic initiation, and tried to avoid the traps of legalism. We've done all this, but still the question remains: ''Am I saved?'' As I said before, there's no reason why you shouldn't *know* you're saved. If you have any doubts whatsoever, now's the time to get rid of them. You can do that by following a simple four-step approach to salvation. This approach is a breakdown of the basic message Jesus taught; it's thoroughly Christian and thoroughly Catholic.

STEP 1 — GOD'S CALL

If you've grasped the basic message of this book, you've already taken step 1. You took it the moment you realized that you're called to have *peace* and *life* in union with your heavenly Father. So let's take a moment and review that call. St. Paul said:

> . . . we are at peace with God through our Lord Jesus Christ.
>
> *Romans 5:1*

Yes, our call is to peace with God our Father through a personal relationship. And that same relationship allows us to function as God always intended us to function. It makes us victorious in this life and gives us life eternal:

> Yes, God so loved the world that he gave his only Son, that whoever believes in him may not die but may have *eternal life.*
>
> *John 3:16*

Jesus went on to emphasize that this "life" was not just barely sufficient, but abundant life:

> I came that they might have life and have it *to the full.*
>
> *John 10:10*

So life in union with the Father should show vitality, strength and inner peace — a superabundance of God's love.

Let's face it, most people you see don't show any evidence of this divine life. They don't experience the Father's love and therefore they're not able to show genuine love to their fellow men. The reason for this sad state of affairs is found in Step 2.

STEP 2 — SEPARATION

In this step you must acknowledge that man is sinful, and that because he's sinful, he has separated himself from God. The Father created man with a very precious gift: a free will. Rather than act like a robot, man could make a free choice. History shows that even the most holy men, at one time or another, chose to rebel against the Father's way of doing things. That rebellion is what we call "sin" and no human being is without these seeds of defiance. St. Paul said:

144

All men have sinned and are deprived of the glory of God.

Romans 3:23

In the Father's mind, sin and separation are exactly the same. And this separation from God has some very practical results, namely, men are unable to get along with their fellow men. You see, only ''in the Father'' can men learn to relate to one another properly; men cannot learn this on their own. Speaking about the sinfulness of men, St. Paul wrote to the Church at Rome:

They did not see fit to acknowledge God, so God delivered them up to their own depraved sense to do what is unseemly. They are filled with every kind of wickedness: maliciousness, greed, ill will, envy, murder, bickering, deceit, craftiness.

Romans 1:28-29

Now perhaps you can begin to see an important point. War and injustice are not the Father's Will. Men, because of sin and separation, have authored these evils. God cannot stop wars, hate, poverty, etc., without interfering directly with our free will, a thing he would never do. So death is the price paid for this rebellion:

The wages of sin is death, but the gift of God is eternal life in Christ Jesus our Lord.

Romans 6:23

Now in the New Testament sin is looked upon not only as individual acts against the Father's Will, but also as a *condition;* let's call it the "state of sinfulness." In this state men are living for their own ends; not really trying to follow the Father's Will. While in the state of sinfulness (separation) anything they do, whether good or bad, does not please the Father. Here's an illustration:

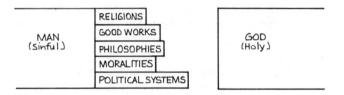

Men have been trying since time began to bridge the gap that sin creates. Their methods include religions, good works, philosophies, moralities and political systems. None have worked — nor will they ever work. The gap will not be bridged and men will not live together in love and peace until there's a fundamental spiritual change which only the Father can produce. Step 3 explains how the Father made such a change possible.

STEP 3 — JESUS CHRIST

Jesus was the Father's answer to the separation problem — not simply his coming but his death, resurrection and Holy Spirit. These bridged the gap, reuniting God and man.

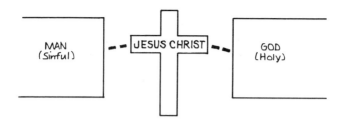

. . . God is on one side and all the people on the other side, and Christ Jesus, Himself man, is between them to bring them together.

1 Timothy 2:5 (Living Bible)

Now there's a very important point here. Jesus did the work of bridging the gap, not you. All your religious activities, good works, alms giving, etc., will in themselves do nothing to bridge that gap. They may be good and proper things to do, but the Father's gift of Jesus is free. You can't earn it. St. Paul said:

I repeat, it is owing to his favor that salvation is yours through faith. This is not your own doing, it is God's gift; neither is it a reward for anything you have accomplished, so let no one pride himself on it.

Ephesians 2:8-9

St. Leo the Great echoed Paul by saying:

Not for any merit of our own, but through the blood of Christ and the free gift of God's grace, we have been healed and set free. What the Lord asks of us now is *not to try to earn* this freedom, but to hold fast to what he has already given us and to guard it from the devil's envy.

Anne Field, O.S.B., *The Binding of the Strong Man,* p. 99.

The point is this: if you had done XXX number of good works to earn salvation, you'd be quite proud of it and pride itself is the root of all sin. Therefore, Jesus comes to you (a sinner) and offers a way to abundant life which doesn't require you to become a new person *before* being saved. No, Jesus comes to save you while you're still steeped in sin. St. Paul pointed out how this *proves* the Father's love:

It is precisely in this that God *proves his love* for us: that while we were *still sinners,* Christ died for us.

Romans 5:8

This fact is very humbling. I often think it would be easier if I had something really hard to do first. But the Father says no, Jesus Christ is the bridge to salvation. So Jesus, repeating what he heard the Father say, proclaimed to all:

I am the way, and the truth, and the life; no one comes to the Father but through me.

John 14:6

Believing this basic Christian truth is an important step. Yet you need do something more than just believe in Jesus Christ. Step 4 explains what must be done.

STEP 4 — ACCEPT AND RECEIVE

This step consists of accepting Jesus Christ as Lord and Savior of your own life, and then receiving the "new life" which the Father wants to give. It's best if we look at "accepting" and "receiving" as separate topics.

Accepting

Now it's essential that you realize the difference between "accepting" Jesus Christ and merely "believing" in him. The New Testament emphasizes that believing is not enough. The epistle of James asks:

> Do you believe that God is one? You are quite right. The demons believe that, and shudder.
>
> *James 2:19*

Someone once suggested that only believing in God's existence qualifies you for nothing more than being one of Satan's agents. The point of St. James' argument — and the point I wish to make here — is that you must *act* upon your belief to accept Jesus Christ. Act how? Well, the first action consists in making Jesus Christ *truly* Lord of your life. Let me illustrate this by drawing three circles. Each circle represents the circle of interest and influence in a person's life.

Person A might be described as the average non-Christian. There are many things in his life, but Jesus Christ is not one of them. Jesus falls outside the circle of influence as represented by the cross drawn outside.

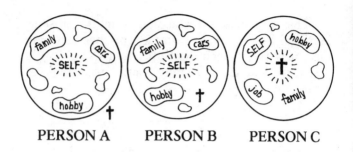

PERSON A   PERSON B   PERSON C

Copyright 1966, Campus Crusade for Christ Inc.

Person B is a Christian by name. Along with all the other things in his life, a certain amount of time is devoted to Christianity (like an hour or two each Sunday morning). Jesus Christ has a certain influence here, but like his friend Person A, ''Self'' is at the center.

Now Person C is a committed Christian. While there are many things in his circle of influence, Jesus Christ is the center and the gospel of Jesus influences every aspect of his life. Jesus isn't just tacked on, Jesus actually *is* his life. As Person C's heavenly brother, Jesus leads him to know the Father through a personal relationship. In the scriptural sense, only Person C has really *accepted* Jesus. And Scripture promises:

Any who did accept him he empowered to become children of God.

John 1:12

150

Receiving

Scripture gives us these words of Jesus:

> Here I stand, knocking at the door. If anyone
> hears me calling and opens the door, I will
> enter his house and have supper with him, and
> he with me.
>
> *Revelation 3:20*

This is an important and powerful principle. Jesus
is knocking, asking, desiring to enter your life; yet you
hold the key. Why do you hold it and not Jesus who is
Lord? Because the Father has given you that most precious gift, *free will.* He cannot violate free will no matter how much he longs to have you become his son or
daughter. So to receive what Jesus offers (divine life),
you must open the door to your inner self. Then and
only then can life come in. Only then can it begin to
transform and empower you. This "divine life" has a
name and personality all its own: it's called the *Holy
Spirit.* He supplies the power to live the committed
Christian life, and without his power your life as a
Christian is bound to be mediocre.

There's a great deal of talk these days about what it
really means to "receive" the Holy Spirit. I'll discuss
that topic in the next chapter. But the point I wish to
make clear now is that you must open the door and let
the Holy Spirit come in; let him empower you to live
the Christian life; let him begin the transformation
which will eventually bring you into complete union
with the Father. Only God's Spirit can accomplish
this, and only if *you* let him. To those who wanted to
know how a person goes about "receiving" salvation,
St. Peter said:

You must reform and be baptized, each one of you, in the name of Jesus Christ, that your sins may be forgiven; then you will *receive the gift of the Holy Spirit.*

Acts 2:38

THE DOING

So much for the principles of "accepting" and "receiving." Now let's put these principles into practice. There are four things you must *do* to come into this relationship we've been talking about. Remember, we're going beyond the minimum for salvation in order to come into a personal relationship with the Father, through Jesus, by means of the Holy Spirit. These are the four actions:

1. *Admit* that you're a sinner and need the forgiving mercy of a loving Father. For Catholics, the Sacrament of Penance is the best place to do this.
2. *Confess* true *repentance* by deciding to completely turn away from sin. Be sincere and trust the Father to supply you with the power needed to carry out your commitment.
3. *Believe* that Jesus Christ *is* who he says he is and believe that through his dying on the cross your sins *are* forgiven. He said they are, so believe him.
4. *Make* Jesus Lord of your life. Let him have control — be the center of influence. You can do this best by *sincerely* reciting the following prayer of commitment. Read it over once and think about it for a minute or two. Then pray with both your heart and your head. It could

be the most important prayer you'll ever say.

Lord Jesus Christ, I acknowledge that I'm a sinner and sincerely need your love and forgiveness. I commit myself to your ways and turn away from all wrongdoing. I believe you died to wipe out the effects of my sins, so I now invite you to come into my life and become Lord. I ask you to empower me now with your Holy Spirit that I may live as a committed Christian. Thank you, Lord.

Remember the words of St. Leo:

No one is refused on account of sin, because to be born again and put right with God is not something to be earned; it is a free gift.

Anne Field, O.S.B., *The Binding of the Strong Man,* p. 57.

and again the words of St. Paul:

He who calls you is trustworthy, therefore he will do it.

1 Thessalonians 5:24

He's in you at this moment. Believe it — it's true! The Father himself said so:

When you call me, when you go to pray to me, I will listen to you. When you look for me, you will find me. Yes, when you seek me with all your heart, you will find me with you, says the Lord.

Jeremiah 29:12-14

CHAPTER 6

There's More

Through these Tennessee hills there travels an old story of the wood-cutting mountain-man. It seems he learned about a new-fangled invention called a ''chainsaw'' and headed to town to buy one.

''Guaranteed to cut you six cord-o-wood a day,'' the salesman promised, ''Just return it if it don't.''

Well the mountain-man returned a few days later — mad as could be. ''Here's yar no-good chainsaw. Worked ma fingers to the bone and only cut me four cord a day.''

The salesman shook his head, ''Don't understand it — that's our best saw. Here, let me try it.'' He pulled the cord and the saw roared to life spitting out a cloud of blue smoke.

Startled, the mountain-man jumped back, ''What's that noise? What's that noise?''

Now you and I often behave like that mountain-man who didn't know the saw contained its own power. We forget that our Christianity is also self-propelled, so we push ahead, trying to do all that Jesus said using our own human strength. But the Father really wants us to use the energy he has provided through our relationship with him.

And there's something really unique about that power: it won't quit — there's always another helping. Some years ago Fr. Dennis J. Bennett wrote a book entitled *There's More*. His message was simply this: in God's Kingdom you'll always find more power, more blessings, more experiences, more God waiting to be discovered. No matter where you are in your Christian walk, you can be excited in knowing the Father has much, much more for you.

As I said before, this inexhaustible power comes from the Holy Spirit. But how does it come? And when? And how do I activate it? And what will it do for me when I do activate it? These are the questions we'll answer in this chapter.

WHAT HAPPENED BEFORE

Let's take another quick look at your Baptism and Confirmation. In the last chapter we talked about these sacraments in relation to being saved. Now we'll look at them in terms of receiving the power of the Holy Spirit. You see, the Holy Spirit is given both in Baptism and Confirmation, but Confirmation is where the power is supposed to ''come alive.'' For many Catholics that simply didn't happen. So let's explore the reasons why it didn't, and learn what we can do to make it happen.

''Wait just one minute,'' you'll protest, ''are you saying that I received the Holy Spirit in Baptism and Confirmation but didn't receive his full empowering?'' Yes, that's exactly what I'm saying. You see, all sacraments require a mature faith to be activated. The Holy Spirit met you where you were in faith at that time and worked with you accordingly. But until your faith matures, you can't expect full empowering.

155

In my own Confirmation, for example, I was only concerned with what the Bishop might ask me and how hard I was going to be hit. I didn't have expectant faith. And even if I did have that faith, a twelve-year-old is hardly mature enough to handle the full power of the Holy Spirit. My faith and I needed to grow up.

After I had grown up, there was still another problem — I simply didn't know that the Holy Spirit's power was available to me as a result of those childhood sacraments. The power just sat there unused. Let me illustrate this. I have many electrical outlets in my house. If you were to trace the wires to the source of the power, you'd discover a vast power-generating system called the Tennessee Valley Authority (TVA). Now TVA has giant steam plants, hydroelectric dams, and nuclear power plants, all working to supply my outlets with electrical energy anytime I need it. But I must do something to get that energy. First, I must believe the power is there for my use and second, I have to act in faith by *plugging in* to the outlet. So if your Baptism and Confirmation were valid, the Holy Spirit in you is like an electrical outlet. He may sit there for years without ever being used because to use the vast power system of the Father, you have to act in mature faith and "plug in" to the Spirit's power.

THE POWERFUL POWER

Now you have it on good authority that the Holy Spirit brings power. Just before he ascended Jesus said that you would

> . . . receive *power* when the *Holy Spirit* comes down on you.

Acts 1:8

But what kind of spiritual power was Jesus talking about? A vague, theological power perhaps? Well it's quite easy to understand what type of power when you learn that the New Testament was originally written in Greek and the word we translate as "power" in this passage was, in Greek, *dunamis*. It's the same word from which we derive our English "dynamite." In other words, it's a power you can easily observe; it's dynamic and effective, even explosive. That's what the Holy Spirit brings — nothing less.

So if there's one sin we're all guilty of, it's underestimating what the Father can do *in us* through the power of the Holy Spirit. St. Paul recognized this problem when he wrote about a Father

> . . . whose *power* now at work *in us* can do *immeasurably more* than we ask or imagine.
>
> *Ephesians 3:20*

In that same letter Paul talks about

> . . . the *immeasurable scope of his power in us* who believe. It is like the strength he showed in raising Christ from the dead.
>
> *Ephesians 1:19-20*

Yet we find many people today who believe this spiritual power is rather vague and hard to detect. These people seem to think that because they're spiritually weak, the Holy Spirit must also be weak. They would have a hard time convincing St. Paul of that. In fact, he noted that it was specifically because we are weak that the Holy Spirit is given to us:

157

The Spirit too *helps us in our weakness.*

Romans 8:26

St. Paul knew of a spiritual power so strong that men were completely transformed whenever they encountered it. There was no mistaking its presence; anyone could see the results. The Acts of the Apostles describes Simon, a man so ignorant of spiritual matters that he offered Peter money for the ability to give the Holy Spirit to others. Yet even Simon could *see* the power:

> Simon *observed* that it was through the laying on of hands that the apostles conferred the Spirit.
>
> *Acts 8:18*

Yes, in each and every account in the Acts of the Apostles where the Holy Spirit descended upon someone or some group, even the most casual observer could see that something happened.

Today we can be transformed in the same way and again the results will be visible. But why shouldn't they be? The Holy Spirit hasn't changed! The Father is using the *power* of his Spirit to bring us into a personal relationship with himself. And by becoming sons of God we can enter, here and now, the ''Kingdom of God.'' Now that's something everyone should notice.

Remember not to confuse the ''Kingdom of God'' with ''heaven.'' As I said before, the Kingdom of God is both in heaven and right here on earth for anyone involved in a personal relationship with the Father. St. Paul describes a few things about this ''Kingdom'':

158

The Kingdom of God does not consist in talk
but in *power.*

1 Corinthians 4:20

The Kingdom of God is not a matter of eating
or drinking, but of justice, peace, and the joy
that is given *by the Holy Spirit.*

Romans 14:17

These two scriptural passages tell you a great deal
about this personal relationship with the Father (who
is King of that Kingdom). It will not consist of definitions and doctrines but of real power, through the
Holy Spirit. That same Spirit gives righteousness,
peace and joy based on this new relationship. Yes, all
those passages where Jesus refers to the "Kingdom of
God" actually describe, not heaven, but a Christian
life *empowered* by the Holy Spirit.

So the Christian character you couldn't produce by
human power will now be produced by the Spirit's
power. St. Paul lists the characteristics of your new
"Spirit-powered" personality:

> . . . the fruit of the spirit is love, joy, peace, pa-
> tient endurance, kindness, generosity, faith,
> mildness, and chastity.

Galatians 5:22

In all this you see a Father who truly cares for you
personally. He gives you, free of charge, a personal intimate relationship. Then he provides the power to
"live out" all that this relationship demands. You
never have to worry about doing it on your own, the
Father has seen to that.

LIVING FAITH

Obviously you need this spiritual power, but exactly how do you go about activating it? How do you make it "come alive?" The answer is faith; you must be a man or woman of faith. But faith is one of the most misunderstood and abused terms in Christianity. Some people will tell you faith means the same thing as belief. It does not! Others will say faith is a set of doctrines and Church dogmas. However, the New Testament says that faith is much more than belief, and it's certainly not a mere set of doctrines. The letter to the Hebrews offers this definition of faith:

> To have faith is to be sure of the things we hope for, to be certain of the things we cannot see.
>
> *Hebrews 11:1 (TEV)*

In other words, faith is a deep abiding *trust* in who your Father is. You know the Father has promised certain things, and you trust him because he's *trustworthy;* he will fulfill those promises. You may not see him doing it right at the moment but because he said it, you believe. People have in the past, and will continue in the future, to let you down; but the Father will not. So faith means responding to his promise by saying: "Yes, Father, I believe what you say and I'm ready to step out and act upon your promise." Remember St. Paul's words:

> He who calls us is *trustworthy*, therefore he will do it.
>
> *1 Thessalonians 5:24*

What sort of action are you taking then? In effect you're surrendering your independent spirit to a Father you can count on to give "more than you ask or imagine" *(Ephesians 3:20)*. Father Brennan Manning has written:

> Whenever faith is accepted merely as a closed system of well-defined dogmas, we lose contact with the living God. The faith that saves is *a surrender* to God.
>
> *Prophets and Lovers,* p. 31.

Now most people understand that the Father supplies "grace" or "power" for faith, but they're not sure how they should "surrender" to him. Well, when you talk about "faith" in connection with a personal relationship you see that, for the most part, surrender takes on the meaning of *total trust*. Jesus clearly told us to trust the Father for all things:

> Ask, and you will receive. Seek, and you will find. Knock, and it will be opened to you. For the one who asks, receives. The one who seeks, finds. The one who knocks, enters. Would one of you hand his son a stone when he asks for a loaf, or a poisonous snake when he asks for a fish? If you, with all your sins, know how to give your children what is good, *how much more* will your heavenly Father give good things to anyone who asks him!
>
> *Matthew 7:7-11*

Now you can understand why a religion that includes "Christian experience" is so important. Trust must be "lived out" through real experiences if it's to grow. If you don't experience the Father's hand guiding you each and every day, you'll never really learn to trust him as you should; you'll never surrender your independence. Please don't fool yourself. Intellectual ''belief'' and real trust are miles apart. If faith remains only an intellectual exercise, it will eventually die. It must be exercised by ''walking in trust'' with the Father. Read the gospels carefully and look at the trusting relationship Jesus had with the Father. Notice how Jesus constantly tried to teach his disciples to have that same trusting faith:

> Again I tell you, if two of you join your voices on earth to pray for anything whatever, it shall be granted you by my Father in heaven. Where two or three are gathered in my name, there am I in their midst.
>
> *Matthew 18:19-20*

In commenting upon Gospel faith, Father Brennan Manning points out:

> In the magnificent sixth chapter of Matthew's Gospel, faith is described as the unconditional acceptance of the God revealed by Jesus Christ as loving Father. Unless we surrender in faith to his saving truth and live buoyed up by its assurance, we have not made the Christian profession of faith. The term ''Father'' occurs eleven times in this one chapter, and it is in this Father that the disciples of Jesus are to place unwavering trust. The disciples are called men of *''little faith'' if they do not trust* their Father who knows their needs and provides for the birds of the air and the lilies of the field.
>
> *Prophets and Lovers*, p. 24.

Developing this kind of trust demands *commitment*. Until Jesus is Lord of your life in the sense we talked about in the last chapter, you'll find it impossible to grow in trusting faith. There's simply no other way — you must make Jesus Christ and his teachings the central focus of your life. Only then will you be able to enjoy a trusting personal relationship. In his book, *Christ Among Us,* Anthony Wilhelm explains this connection between faith and commitment:

> Faith is ultimately a *commitment,* a free choice by which we give ourselves to Christ and begin living a whole new way of life. It is a free and personal decision to abandon ourselves to the living God. We are converted, we turn fully toward him, a changed person.
>
> Faith is perhaps best looked at as a dynamic *relationship,* a living and continual encounter between God and oneself, by which we continually grow in knowledge of him and his will for us, and *commit* ourselves to live by this.
>
> *Christ Among Us,* p. 204.

So this living faith we're talking about is a surrender of our independent ''I can take care of myself'' attitude. It's a deep trust in the Father based upon our total commitment. This kind of faith is best called ''expectant faith.'' It's a faith that believes, trusts and *expects* things to happen. Expectant faith is the faith Jesus taught:

> I give you my word, if you are *ready to believe* that you will receive whatever you ask for in prayer, it shall be done for you.
>
> *Mark 11:24*

Expectant faith believes what the Father has said — believes his covenants and promises — and not only believes but acts upon what it believes. It steps out to say, "Father, you said it, I believe it, that settles it." It's bold, gutsy, uncompromising. It never cops out by adding, "Well, of course, if it be your will." Expectant faith knows for sure what his will is, and acts accordingly.

POWER THROUGH EXPECTANT FAITH

So how do you activate the power of the Holy Spirit? Simply ask! But ask in expectant faith. Believe the Father; he said he wants to empower you with his Spirit. Believe and expect it to happen. If anyone can be trusted, your heavenly Father can. Hear again the words of Jesus:

> As bad as you are, you know how to give good things to your children. How much more, then, the Father in heaven will give the Holy Spirit to those who ask him.
>
> *Luke 11:13 (TEV)*

If you read through the Gospels, you'll find that no one ever came to Jesus *in faith* asking for anything, and was turned away. Jesus always met their needs. So now the Father, through Jesus, has told you to ask for the Spirit's empowering; it should be easy for you to approach this promise with expectant faith. And not only should you expect the Father to do what he has promised, but you also should expect to see some sign of it. You should expect a definite manifestation of the Spirit's power at work in you. It doesn't necessarily have to be a certain type feeling, or a particular gift of

164

the Spirit, or anything else that someone you know has experienced. There is always a bit of mystery in the way the Holy Spirit empowers a person. Don't tie him down by expecting him to act in any particular way. Release him! But do expect to see his presence in a very concrete way.

If you feel you've never exercised "expectant faith," if you feel you've never experienced the Spirit's power in your life, use the simple prayer below to activate that untapped power. Remember, your prayer must be sincere — it must come from your heart. Read it through a couple of times, think about it and then really pray it.

Beloved Father, I've committed myself to you and made Jesus Christ the Lord of my life. Now I desire to deepen this personal relationship with you and so I need the power of your Holy Spirit which you've promised to give me. Father release that power within me now, and let me experience that presence through some sign of your love. Thank you Father — so shall it be.

FEELINGS

The presence of the Spirit in you often brings feelings of love, joy, peace, patience, etc. — all the fruits of the Holy Spirit. But you must never depend upon these or any other particular feeling as a sign that the Holy Spirit is, or is not, present. If you've been baptized and confirmed, if you've made a sincere request for the empowering of the Holy Spirit, then you *must believe* that it will happen. After all, the Father himself promised it.

Let's look at this problem of feelings for a moment. The Father has revealed certain "facts" about himself and about your relationship with him. You accept these facts based on "faith." Your feelings or emotions come after your act of faith. Consider this illustration:

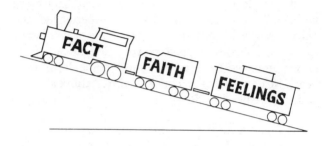

Copyright 1966, Campus Crusade for Christ Inc.

The Father's revelation of *fact* is the source of power and strength here. *Faith* follows behind and supplies the raw material (fuel) to produce that power. *Feelings* trail behind — in fact they could be left off entirely and the train would still move. Feelings are a comfort and it's certainly a great joy to "feel" the presence of God. You should want feelings, but they can't drive the train and they shouldn't drive you to accept or reject what the Father has promised. If they come along — great! If they don't, faith based on fact tells you that everything is still in fine shape. If you have honestly and sincerely prayed for the empowering of the Holy Spirit, then you should believe it has happened. That's a *fact*.

PROBLEMS IN RECEIVING

I'll be perfectly honest with you; many people have a problem when it comes to receiving or activating the full power of the Holy Spirit. They pray, plead, analyze and repent but it still doesn't come. You'll hear them say, "I prayed with expectant faith, I repented as well as I know how, but I still don't think anything happened. Not only are there no feelings, I can't see any fruits either."

There's a great temptation at this point to just quit. If you're having such a problem, I'm asking you not to give in to that temptation. Instead let's try to unearth that block — let's get the Spirit's power working for you.

Now there are a number of things that can prevent the release of that power. So ask yourself these questions:

Have I really surrendered?

You'll find your free will is a lot stronger than you ever imagined. You may find that it's preventing you from surrendering — from making that commitment we spoke of earlier. If you're holding out in any area, you haven't made Jesus "Lord" of that area. Remember, he's asking for *total* surrender. Cardinal Suenens comments:

I have to examine myself, ask some direct questions: "Am I really converted? Do I honestly have my *whole* soul turned toward the Lord in a true metanoia? Am I content with keeping clear of overt sin and calling this conversion, while at the same time clinging to a wisdom that is all my own, my own ideas, my prudence, my notions of how things

should be? Have I really accepted Jesus as my
Lord in all the concrete events of my life?''

A New Pentecost?, p. 133.

Is my pride preventing surrender?

To surrender takes humility, and none of us have
an overabundance of that virtue. Don't confuse shy-
ness and timidity with humility. True Christian humility allows us to have a servant's heart — to serve God
and our fellow man. Often you'll find that even the
most shy person has a great deal of inward pride. So no
matter what your personality, you should examine
your sense of pride; it may be excessive and therefore
blocking true surrender.

Do I harbor unforgiveness?

Unforgiveness is perhaps the biggest obstacle
preventing the Father from pouring his Spirit into
your life; essentially it puts a damper on the Holy
Spirit's action. Jesus was well aware of this, and after
giving the Lord's prayer, he significantly chose to emphasize one point:

> If you forgive the faults of others, your
> heavenly Father will forgive you yours. If you
> do not forgive others, neither will your Father
> forgive you.
>
> *Matthew 6:14-15*

Through practical experience I've found that unforgiveness is a common block for people asking anything of the Father. The problem usually centers
around some ''unforgiveable'' event in the past which
really hurts. They fail to realize that forgiveness is a
decision of the mind — not an emotion. Often they
must simply decide to forgive, and ignore their emo-

tions altogether. After a time the emotion of forgiveness catches up with the decision and these people can actually feel forgiveness for that past hurt.

If you have any unforgiveness in you, the Father will be asking you to get rid of it. He can't act in and through you as he would like until it's been gotten rid of. He'll ask you to *decide* to forgive. Forget about your emotions. They may be shouting ''I can't forgive,'' but that's a lie. Forgiveness is a decision — you can make it. St. Leo said:

> Although this business of forgiving others is so demanding and difficult for us, it is at the same time a tremendous joy to know that the Lord uses it to heal our own wounds. How often we need forgiveness ourselves for the innumerable faults we fall into! And here we are given the key to it: when we forgive our brother, the Lord forgives us. When we show compassion to others, we ourselves experience the compassion of the Lord.

Anne Field, O.S.B., *The Binding of the Strong Man, pp. 66-67.*

Do I lack real trust?

The Spirit will ask you to develop a constant awareness that you've given the Father complete charge. No matter what the circumstances may be, he's at the controls and has allowed you to experience both ''good'' and ''bad,'' both pain and joy. St. Paul's words to the Romans will be your motto:

> We know that God makes *all things* work together *for the good* of those who have been called according to his decree.

Romans 8:28

169

Only through difficulties and trials will you really learn to trust your Father. The trust he desires is a mature trust, taking time and experience to grow. It starts with the attitude that God is a Father *who can be trusted indeed.*

"But how do I know I've developed enough trust?" you'll ask. Well, when you're really acting as a trusting son or daughter and accepting all things as being for your good, you'll begin to praise the Father for all things. Yes, even when things are (in the ordinary sense) not working out well, you praise and thank him. Why? Because you're a son or daughter who knows he has allowed it, and eventually you'll see the good in it. Here is a scripture passage worth memorizing:

> *Rejoice always,* never cease praying, render *constant thanks;* such is God's will for you in Christ Jesus.
>
> 1 Thessalonians 5:16

Yes, even in the face of your worst troubles, you must thank the Father. This attitude of "constant thanks" releases the Holy Spirit's power. It doesn't remove the problem, but brings you through with supernatural strength. Believe me, it works.

Do I expect the extraordinary?

You may be blocking the Spirit's power because you expect *too little.* The Father is a "supernatural" God, so don't make the mistake of restricting him to the ordinary. Some gifts of the Holy Spirit are, to say the least *unusual.* But when you really think about it, shouldn't it be that way? There's certainly nothing plain and ordinary about God's very life coursing through your being. There's nothing ordinary about a human being taking on immortality. Cardinal Suenens writes:

> We might be tempted to distinguish two kinds of experience: one ordinary, the other extraordinary. Such a distinction is false. It is based on our way of judging, in so far as the meeting with God seemed, or did not seem, in our view, to be unexpected, unusual or unique. But this is foreign to God's way of judging.
>
> For God there is no line of demarcation between "ordinary" and "extraordinary." He crosses with ease the dotted line that marks *our* frontiers. In God the extraordinary is ordinary.

A New Pentecost?, p. 64.

Am I patient enough?

Finally, if everything seems to be in order, you must simply be patient. Often after a prayer for the Spirit's empowering there's a delayed reaction. It could be a matter of minutes, hours, or even days. Relax, begin to exercise that trust you need to develop, and most important, *expect* something to happen. It surely will.

THE TRINITY WHIRLWIND

Now you should expect to see the Holy Spirit performing one special mission in every Christian. Jesus tells us exactly what that mission is:

> When he comes, however, being the Spirit of truth he will guide you to all truth. He will not speak on his own, but will speak only what he

hears, and will announce to you the things to come. In doing this he will give glory to me, because he will have received from me what he will announce to you. All that the Father has belongs to me. That is why I said that what he will announce to you he will have from me.

John 16:13-15

In commenting on this work of the Holy Spirit, Cardinal Suenens writes:

The special mission of the Spirit is to reveal not himself, but Jesus, the unique Son of God. Within each Christian heart, the Spirit is faithful to this mission: he accompanies us step by step, shedding on our path, as we advance in faith, a light from within.

A New Pentecost?, p. 55.

The Spirit, then, reveals Jesus. It is Jesus who, in turn, shows you how to enter into and grow in a personal relationship with the Father. The Father in turn sends the Spirit, who reveals Jesus, who leads to the Father, who etc. Now you begin to understand that you're using this power of the Spirit to enter the very life-cycle of the Trinity; you're caught up in the whirlwind of God's love and power. Now that's exciting.

Now you can understand why it's easy to detect the Holy Spirit's action within you; it's actually part of the life-substance of the Trinity. As I said before, it's "explosive." Jesus told us what to expect:

John baptized with water, but within a few days you will be *baptized* with the Holy Spirit.

Acts 1:5

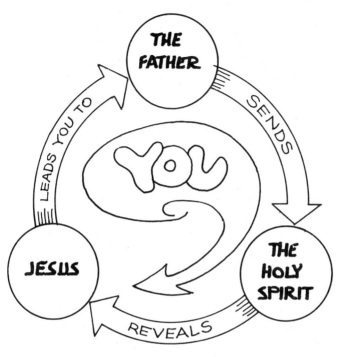

Now in those days Baptism meant total immersion. So to be "baptized in the Holy Spirit" means to be immersed, saturated, filled to overflowing with God's Spirit. That's why receiving the Holy Spirit was always so "visible" in the Acts of the Apostles. It had to be! The power of the Father filling a person is dramatic. Your job as a committed Christian, therefore, must be to seek a deeper experience of the Holy Spirit's power each and every day. Pray earnestly for all the "gifts and fruits of the Spirit." Pray that the Spirit will reveal Jesus more clearly so that Jesus in turn can lead you into a deeper personal relationship with the Father. Pray for the Spirit's full empowering.

THE BOTTOM LINE

When a businessman makes a financial deal he always wants to know, ''What's the bottom line — the final cost?'' He may ask about discounts, payments, interest, etc., but what really counts is that old bottom line. Now you're probably thinking the very same thing about this new life and power in the Holy Spirit: ''What's the Father's bottom line?''

Well, if you'll recall that diagram we used in the last chapter (page 141) describing the purgative process, you'll remember that the narrow road leads to union with the Father. But before that union can take place, you must be changed — made ''perfect.'' C.S. Lewis wrote:

> That is why He warned people to ''count the cost'' before becoming Christians. ''Make no mistake,'' He says, ''if you let me, I will make you perfect. The moment you put yourself in My hands, that is what you are in for. Nothing less, or other, than that. You have free will, and if you choose, you can push Me away. But if you do not push Me away, understand that I am going to see this job through. Whatever suffering it may cost you in your earthly life, whatever inconceivable purification it may cost you after death, whatever it costs Me, I will never rest, nor let you rest, until you are literally perfect — until my Father can say without reservation that He is well pleased with you, as He said He was well pleased with me. This I can do and will do. But I will not do anything less.''

Mere Christianity, p. 172.

This idea didn't originate with C.S. Lewis. It has been part of Christian teaching since Jesus said: "You must be made perfect" *(Matthew 5:48)*. So a committed Christian has a dual personality. There's the "old man," the "sinful nature," the "natural life" which needs to be transformed; and there's a new life, a supernatural, spiritual life coming from the Father through his Spirit. Again, C.S. Lewis remarks:

> The two kinds of life are now not only different (they would always have been that) but actually opposed. The natural life in each of us is something self-centered, something that wants to be petted and admired, to take advantage of other lives, to exploit the whole universe. And especially it wants to be left to itself: to keep well away from anything better or stronger or higher than it, anything that might make it feel small. It is afraid of the light and air of the spiritual world, just as people who have been brought up to be dirty are afraid of a bath. And in a sense it is quite right. It knows that if the spiritual life gets hold of it, all its self-centeredness and self-will are going to be killed and it is ready to fight tooth and nail to avoid that.
>
> *Mere Christianity*, p. 154.

This dying of the old man is what Jesus was talking about when he said that a person must lose his life if he really wants to find it.

> Whoever would save his life will lose it, but whoever loses his life for my sake will find it.
>
> *Matthew 16:25*

So God's bottom line is an inevitable struggle between his Holy Spirit transforming you and your old nature fighting his work. You, with your free will, stand between the two judging which will win. Yes, that's right, you will do the judging. The Holy Spirit is a gentleman — he won't force any changes.

And remember, you are not on the "doing" end in this struggle, but on the "yielding" and "receiving" end. You *receive* an invitation to change, you *yield* your free will and you *receive* the Spirit's power to carry out that decision. That's why St. Paul told you to "be transformed" when he wrote:

> Do not conform yourselves to this age but *be transformed* by the renewal of your mind, so that you may judge what is God's will, what is good, pleasing and perfect.
>
> *Romans 12:2*

I'm glad I'm not expected to make the changes myself. I couldn't do it. But with the Spirit's power working for me, I know I'll become what the Father desires. Praise God for his Holy Spirit.

FELLOWSHIP

Once you open up to the Holy Spirit, experience his power and perhaps feel his presence, you'll want even more. There's a problem, though, with the Father giving you all you desire. It would be like giving a youngster control of a powerful racing car — he simply couldn't handle all that energy without experience. Someone surely would get hurt. So the Father will see to it that you receive only what you can handle.

Now there's one way you can quickly learn to handle more of the Holy Spirit's power, and that's by participating in the proper type of fellowship. This will provide you with control and direction, allowing the Father to give you ever-increasing power. But now you run into another problem: such fellowship is hard to find. Yes, close Christian fellowship where the Holy Spirit's power is working is a very rare thing. Contrast this to the early Church where:

> They spent their time in learning from the apostles, taking part in the fellowship, and sharing in the fellowship meals and the prayers.
>
> *Acts 2:42 (TEV)*

Our normal Church life should supply that fellowship, but it doesn't. The average Catholic parish today falls far short of the kind of Christian community we need. Too many people come to "put in" their one hour a week. A recent survey showed that only 12% of the average Catholic parish was really "active." But even being counted among the 12% doesn't mean you'll have the Christian fellowship you need. A person can spend all his available time in parish "activities" and never be part of the type of Christian fellowship that provides growth. So your best alternative is to search for a group that can supply it. There are certain things you must look for in such a group. It should:

1. Believe in a personal relationship with the Father.
2. Center its activities on helping members develop that relationship.

3. Provide a format in meetings to discuss how the Father is working in your life.
4. Provide teaching and books to help you in your spiritual growth.
5. Meet at least once a week.

In the Catholic Church today there are only two wide-spread movements which meet these criteria: the Cursillo and the Charismatic Renewal. There may indeed be others, but only these two are international in scope.

The Cursillo movement began in Spain in 1949 and has spread throughout the world. Those involved are first asked to make a special closed retreat. During this retreat laymen and priests give participants a "short course" in practical Christianity and introduce them to a personal relationship with the Father. This initial retreat is followed up by other meetings, the most important of which are weekly meetings in small groups to discuss each person's spiritual growth. This movement has been encouraged at all levels of the Church, even by the Pope himself. Almost every diocese in the country has a Cursillo coordinator and if you need information about this movement, you may write to:

The National Cursillo Center
P.O. Box 21226
Dallas, Texas 75211

The Charismatic Renewal, which began in 1967 at Duquesne and Notre Dame Universities, has also spread throughout the world. Cardinal Suenens writes:

The charismatic renewal brings us a new awareness of our spiritual treasures, a new appreciation of our Christian heritage, and new awakening as the people of God.

From an article: ''The First Decade of the Catholic Charismatic Renewal,'' *New Covenant* magazine, Vol. 6, No. 8, February 1977, p. 13.

The Charismatic Renewal emphasizes both a personal relationship with the Father and an openness to the Holy Spirit's power. The term ''charismatic'' stems from the ''charisms'' or ''gifts'' of the Holy Spirit, which participants are actually experiencing. Vatican II stated that these gifts of the Holy Spirit can and should be manifest today (cf. Documents of Vatican II, The Church, #12), even though some have questioned the validity of such manifestations.

Theologians have investigated the Charismatic Renewal and all its aspects and have found it to be a well-balanced presentation of basic Christianity. It has gained so much recognition that Pope Paul VI, in a special audience where both ''Charismatics'' and ''non-Charismatics'' were present, encouraged those not in the movement to join the celebration. Paul VI said:

The second message is for those pilgrims present at this great assembly who do not belong to your movement. They should unite themselves with you to celebrate the feast of Pentecost — the spiritual renewal of the world, of our society, and of our souls — so that they too, devout pilgrims to this center of the Catholic faith, might nourish themselves on the enthusiasm and the spiritual energy with which we must live our religion. And we will say only this: today, either one lives one's faith with devotion, depth, energy, and joy or that faith will die out.

Special audience for the 9th Annual International Conference on the Charismatic Renewal in the Catholic Church, Rome, May 19, 1975, reported in *New Covenant* magazine, Vol. 5, No. 1, July 1975, p. 25.

Most Catholic Charismatic groups provide a place of joyful fellowship as well as an opportunity for one to grow in a personal relationship with God through teaching programs. For more information write:

National Service Committee
237 North Michigan
South Bend, Indiana 46601

If either a Cursillo or a Charismatic group is available to you, join them lest, as Pope Paul said, " . . . that faith will die out." If neither is available, seek others who, like yourself, want to grow in a personal relationship with God. With these brothers and sisters in Christ, share what the Father is doing in your life — both your ups and downs. Discuss what the Father is telling you and seek the spiritual discernment of others. Such fellowship will give you true spiritual strength; it will be a key element in the development of your spiritual life as a whole.

One word of warning here. Don't let fellowship meetings, as essential as they are, interfere with your own personal relationship with God. Your objective is not to become a good participant at meetings, but rather to have such meetings become a tool for deepening your relationship with God. You are now a son or daughter of the Father — not of meetings. Meetings are important, but remember who has called you and

the price he has paid. Your first loyalty is to him.
Father Brennan Manning has written:

> Through the beautiful imagery of the vine and
> the branches, Jesus calls all men to himself.
> "Abide in me, dwell in me, resort to me,
> come to me."
>
> Significantly, Jesus does not say, "Come to a
> day of renewal, a retreat, a prayer meeting, a
> liturgy," but "come to me."

Prophets and Lovers, p. 38.

TEMPTATIONS

Only when you enter into a personal relationship
with the Father will you begin to see and appreciate
Satan's power. There are people today who try to dismiss this idea of a real, personal, evil being; but the
Catholic Church has always taught that he does in fact
exist. Pope Paul VI strongly reaffirmed that Satan is a
real, evil personality — rather than some vague in-
clination of mankind toward evil. Paul VI described
Satan as:

> A living, spiritual being, which is perverted
> and perverts. A terrible *reality* and mysterious
> and fearful. This hidden and disturbing being
> *truly exists* and, with unbelievable cun-
> ningness, still is at work. He is the hidden
> enemy who sows errors and disasters in
> human history.

If you see Satan as the "red devil" with pitchfork
in hand ready to make you do wrong, you place yourself just where he wants you. Why? Because soon you

dismiss him as a fairy tale and go on your merry way. Satan is in fact a powerful spiritual personality with far superior intellect than either you or I possess. He's not against good; but against *God*. He can and will do almost anything to achieve his purpose; and that purpose is to draw men away from the Father and into the kingdom of darkness. Pride and intellectualism are two of his most effective weapons. St. Leo observed:

> Since Satan can achieve nothing against Jesus directly, he uses all his skill to injure those who serve him and to deprive new Christians of the fruits of the Holy Spirit before they have time to reach maturity. He makes some of them swell with pride on account of their intellectual attainments, others he deceives with erroneous opinions, others he so flatters that in their self-righteousness they condemn and persecute everyone else.

> Anne Field, O.S.B., *The Binding of the Strong Man,* p. 48.

Jesus himself was well aware of Satan's power. He spent much time correcting misinterpretations of Jewish theology for his disciples, and it would have been a simple matter to tell them that their idea of Satan as a personality was wrong. He taught many things much harder to take than that. Yet he repeatedly refers to Satan as a real person. He tells his disciples:

> I watched Satan fall from the sky like lightning.

> *Luke 10:18*

Jesus had no doubts about who he was dealing with and neither should you. If you seek to grow in a

182

personal relationship with the Father, Satan will be working against it in any way possible. As long as your Christian life is ineffective, dull and lifeless, he'll leave you alone. But make a commitment to follow Jesus into a personal relationship, and you'll find Satan very concerned. St. Leo wrote:

> Anyone who loves the Lord and tries to live for him is bound to experience the pull of the old Adam as well as the assaults of the devil.
>
> Anne Field, O.S.B., *The Binding of the Strong Man*, p. 90.

Well then, if you can expect to be assaulted, what specifically should you look for? Basically the tactic Satan employs most effectively is doubt. His argument will be that the promise of a personal relationship is pious rhetoric. Read the scriptures and you'll see him applying this weapon over and over again. The temptation of Jesus is a classical example. Satan was asking Jesus to doubt the promise that he was uniquely the only *begotten* son of the Father. In the days of St. Leo the tactic was the same:

> Satan will try to persuade him (the Christian) that the Lord's promise is not true, that God's call is not for him.
>
> Anne Field, O.S.B., *The Binding of the Strong Man*, p. 89.

When these doubts come — and come they will — you should stand firm as Jesus did. He knew what the Father had promised through the scriptures. He quoted the scriptures to Satan and truth defeated evil. Be prepared to do the same. Scripture says:

> All who are led by the Spirit of God are sons of God.
>
> *Romans 8:14*

CHAPTER 7

Signals Over the Badlands

Our flying vacation to the West was well into its second day as we winged our way across South Dakota's Badlands — a colorful expanse of devastated real estate. Mile after mile our eyes gazed upon beautifully eroded hills and canyons, seemingly without life except for patches of prairie grass and an occasional buffalo herd. We had been flying over that well-named wasteland for thirty minutes when I sensed something was wrong. We should have been just west of park headquarters, yet it was nowhere in sight — nothing but endless desolation. My dead-reckoning navigation had failed — we were lost.

I turned to my wife, Sheila. She too is a pilot, so I couldn't hide my problem. "How 'bout getting a cross bearing on our location." I continued to search in vain for landmarks as she dialed in radio frequencies and plotted bearings — 180-deg off Philip VOR, 105-deg off Rapid City. There, she had it. Her finger pointed to the intersection of two penciled lines on the map.

"Good grief! We're twenty miles southeast of where we should be." I banked the plane sharply from its easterly heading and took up a northwesterly track, all the time thanking the Father for modern electronics and a wife who could use them. Within minutes the park headquarters appeared on the horizon.

Reflecting on that experience, I can see its similarity to spiritual guidance. Most Christians expect to fly over life's badlands using their own human abilities, and usually they end up like me — lost and confused. They don't realize that the Father constantly beams spiritual guidance to his sons and daughters; and even those that do realize it don't know how to tune in on his signals. Like my flying experience, they turn for guidance only as a last resort, hoping to get bailed out of a desperate situation.

Americans spend millions every day in psychiatric fees to find out who they are and where they're going — two questions we all must answer one way or another. Yet our Father provides those answers: the personal relationship tells us who we are, and guidance sets us on the right path. Guidance is the whole point of this personal relationship — this born-again experience. That's why Jesus referred to the Holy Spirit as our Paraclete — our guide and counselor. You see, it's inconceivable that a Father who invites us to a personal relationship would not also want to guide us.

Yes, guidance is for real, and the Father wants *all* his children to experience it. In this chapter you'll learn the true sources of guidance, see how they're used and learn ways to avoid problems. But first you need to believe that guidance is yours for the asking.

Today you'll find many people, priests included, who believe direct, personal guidance is not a Christian's privilege. To ignore such guidance they must ignore the teachings of Jesus and the experience of countless saints and holy people throughout Church history. Perhaps they've never earnestly sought personal guidance, and with a skeptical mind, assume that because they haven't experienced it, personal guidance doesn't exist. If only they would hear the words of the Prophet Jeremiah:

> When your words came, I devoured them: your word was my delight and the joy of my heart.
>
> *Jeremiah 15:16 (JB)*

There's no thrill akin to hearing the Father's voice through guidance, and we can only pity those who would shut out his direction through lack of faith or lack of experience.

At the other extreme you find people who believe personal guidance is somehow automatic — you can really just take it for granted. "If you're a Christian," they reason, "guidance will be there somehow even if you don't sense it." That concept is also false. Christian experience throughout 2000 years has shown guidance to be the result of a hungry heart and a mind that seeks truth. St. Paul wrote:

> Do not continue in ignorance, but *try* to discern the will of the Lord.
>
> *Ephesians 5:17*

and again:

> Do not conform yourselves to this age but be transformed by the renewal of your mind, so that *you may judge what is God's will,* what is good, pleasing and perfect.
>
> *Romans 12:2*

The apostle is saying that guidance demands that you work at it. Simply wanting it doesn't produce true guidance. Now there are two initial steps you must take in this pleasant task. First, be a committed Christian in a personal relationship with the Father and second, desire to grow in that relationship. The Father and your relationship with him must be foremost in your mind, for as Proverbs says:

> Trust wholeheartedly in Yahweh, put no faith in *your own perception;* in every course you take, have him in mind: he will see that your paths are smooth.
>
> *Proverbs 3:5-6 (JB)*

In addition to these two essential first steps, you must have available true sources of guidance. So let's look at what the Father has provided and how you can use these sources effectively.

SCRIPTURE

The American Bishops have pointed out that:

> The words of St. Paul should describe the Catholic student of religion: "From your infancy you have known the Sacred Scriptures, the source of the wisdom which, through faith in Jesus Christ, leads to salvation. All Scripture is inspired of God and is useful for teaching — for reproof, correction, and training in holiness . . ." *(2 Timothy 3:16)*
>
> *Basic Teachings for Catholic Religious Education,* Introduction.

Unfortunately few Catholics have this knowledge of Scripture. The Bishops confirm that Catholics need it, yet you must devote time each and every day to Scripture reading to get that knowledge, and if you're a typical Catholic, you're not in the habit of doing that.

I once heard someone say, "Reading Scripture is thinking the thoughts of God after him." In a very real sense that's true; therefore, it illustrates why Scripture is so essential for guidance. With a good working knowledge of Scripture, much "questioning" about the Father's will is unnecessary. You already have it in black and white in the pages of "his Word."

Scriptural principles, you see, must be the jumping off point in this whole area of guidance. For instance, the Church uses Scripture as her guidance foundation:

> The Word of God (Scripture) is life giving. It nourishes and inspires, strengthens and sustains. *It is the primary source,* with Tradition, of Church teaching.
>
> *Basic Teachings for Catholic Religious Education,* Introduction.

Jesus said, "The words I spoke to you are Spirit and life" *(John 6:63).* So the Father's life can only grow if you're working at developing these "scriptural principles." You must constantly read and study the "Father's Word." Note the admonition of St. Jerome: "Ignorance of Scripture is ignorance of Christ."

There are many techniques you can use for scriptural guidance. As I just said, faithful reading of Scripture in itself yields guidance because it deposits inside you a body of truth that is consciously and unconsciously drawn upon. But that storehouse of scriptural knowledge must be constantly reinforced and expanded by study. There's no substitute for it; fifteen minutes a day, every day, is an absolute minimum for scripture reading.

Another technique used in scriptural guidance is sometimes called "scriptural roulette"; it consists of opening the Bible at random and using the first passage you find as a guide. It's a valid means of guidance and has been used throughout the ages by men and women seeking the Father's Will. St. Francis of Assisi used it. However, use of this technique *must be led by the Holy Spirit.* All too often people resort to such techniques because they've neglected prayer, Scripture study, the Sacraments, plus other sources they should normally be cultivating. Scriptural roulette then becomes an *easy out* when things are rough and time is short. If you try this technique, use a great deal of discretion, plenty of prayer and at least two other independent sources of guidance. The Father isn't offended when you seek two other sources. On the contrary, he expects you to follow sound guidance principles.

There are also a variety of "daily scriptural readings" available. You don't have to "pray the Office" to find good daily meditations which the Father can use, and often does, to speak directly about situations you're facing. Again, as with scriptural roulette, be sure you use other sources to confirm any leading.

THE CHURCH'S TEACHINGS

The Church records a long history of men seeking the Father's Will, men who sometimes made mistakes, but who learned from them and wrote the lessons down for others to follow. It would be foolish to ignore this great body of knowledge and experience. The U.S.

Bishops have written that . . .

> . . . the conscience of the Catholic Christian
> must pay respectful and obedient attention to
> the teaching authority of God's Church. It is
> the duty of this teaching authority, or Magis-
> terium, to give *guidance* for applying the en-
> during norms and values of Christian morality
> to specific situations of everyday life.
>
> *Basic Teachings for Catholic Religious Education, #17.*

Any true leading from the Father will not conflict
with true Traditions of the Church established by the
Holy Spirit.

THE SACRAMENTS

Vatican II stated:

> The purpose of the sacraments is to sanctify
> men, to build up the body of Christ, and final-
> ly, to give worship to God. Because they are
> signs *they also instruct.* They not only presup-
> pose faith, but by words and objects they also
> nourish, strengthen, and express it; that is
> why they are called "sacraments of faith."
>
> *Documents of Vatican II,* Constitution on the Sacred
> Liturgy, *#59.*

During Mass the Father's Word is proclaimed
both in scripture readings and sermons. This often is
very direct and powerful guidance. Of course that
doesn't mean that every scripture reading and every
sermon will apply to your specific situation, but the
Father often uses these means to guide his sons and

daughters. Remember, you're dealing with a "sacrament of faith," so you need to approach it with an expectant faith that says, "Father I believe you can and will speak to me in this Mass. Let your word and your truth be proclaimed here."

Now all sacraments communicate something of the Father's will, but the only other sacrament which normally gives direct guidance is Penance. Here the priest speaks the Father's Mind in specific situations where you're obviously having problems. I've often experienced the reality of the Father's love most strongly after receiving this sacrament. Again, it's a "sacrament of faith" and must be approached with an expectant faith which believes that the Father can speak directly through your confessor. Remember, repentance really means to "turn away from" your sins; be committed, therefore, both to hear the Father speak and to act upon his guidance.

CIRCUMSTANCES

The Father often uses various circumstances in a committed Christian's life to communicate guidance. Of course you might have a problem discerning which circumstances are the result of your normal activities, and which are created by the Father to guide or teach you. The danger of mistaking ordinary circumstances for true guidance can be eliminated if you make a point of always using other *independent* sources as a check. In other words, circumstances can and will be used but they must never be used independently.

Let me give you an example of how circumstances are used. The Father had been guiding our local Christian community to seek the advice of another mature community located some sixty miles away in Huntsville, Alabama. We were lax in making contact, so the Father arranged a series of *circumstances* to bring us together.

First my employer sent me to Huntsville for only one day of a three-day technical conference. The morning session ended early, and with an hour to spend before lunch, I decided to scout around the convention center and find the room for the afternoon session. I misread what later proved to be very clear signs and soon became lost in the center's north end. As I turned to retrace my steps a voice rang out, ''Hey Al, what are you doing here?'' It was Mark, a leader of the Huntsville community. We discovered that we both had the next few hours free, so over lunch we made the much-needed plans for the two communities to get together.

We also recounted the circumstances which made our meeting possible. I normally would have been at work sixty miles away. I was attending only one day of a three-day conference, and chose the one session that happened to get out early. I should have been in the room for the afternoon session instead of being lost in that part of the building.

Mark likewise would normally have been elsewhere. He was to help out at the conference the next day, but had stopped by for a few minutes to check last-minute details. Both of us also had time available before afternoon activities would again send us on separate ways. Actually the list of circumstances was longer than I've mentioned here, and the odds against our meeting were apparently astronomical. Yet we both agreed that the Father had arranged *circumstances* in such a way that we were each at the same spot at precisely the same time. The plans we made that day were further proof of the Father's guidance; a valuable conference between the two Christian communities resulted from our discussions.

CHRISTIAN BOOKS

Today there's such a vast number of fine Christian books that you could spend all your time reading and never run out. The Father has inspired men and women to write his thoughts in numerous and varied ways. I've quoted several fine authors in writing this book, yet these only scratch the surface. There are numerous gifted authors who can open areas of the Christian mystery and Scripture which would otherwise lay hidden. As a committed Christian you should continually be reading books that expand your understanding of the Christian life and allow the Father to guide you. The Father uses men and women of all denominations, and you shouldn't feel that only Catholic literature is useful. In fact, I've often found non-Catholic authors speak clearer and more powerfully than Catholic authors. A bibliography is included at the end of this chapter which lists some significant Christian books on today's market. They can greatly aid in developing your personal relationship with God.

PRAYER

Happily, the Church in recent years has been moving away from ideas about prayer that made it a formal, ritualistic chore. Nowadays teaching correctly points to prayer as a *conversation* with our Father. In their "Basic Teachings" document, the U.S. Bishops said that . . .

. . . there is more to prayer than memorized formulas. Talking with God *spontaneously* and *familiarly,* and *listening* to him, is prayer. Informal prayer, suited to the person's age and capacity, should be explained and encouraged. Praise and thankfulness in prayer bring balance and strength in the difficulties, as well as the joys of life.

Basic Teachings for Catholic Religious Education, Introduction.

Prayer, most importantly, has to be *real.* It must come from the heart first — the head second. When you speak with the Father, tell him how you feel — how you *really* feel. If you're happy, tell him. If you're sad and down in the dumps, tell him. If you're mad, let him know about it. Be yourself. After all, he knows your thoughts better than you do. Laugh if you want to; cry if you feel like it. Don't hide your emotions. That's not the way the Father made you and it certainly isn't the way he expects you to act. Cardinal Suenens wrote:

For if someone objects to the emotional character of a particular style of prayer, it can well be that he feels himself threatened by its personal quality. We are so accustomed to formalism, ritualism, and conventionalism, that deeply personal prayer can present a challenge to our inhibitions. We are afraid to be ourselves before God and before one another and hence we resort to a defense mechanism which labels as ''emotionalism'' what in reality is an authentic personal quality of prayer. We tend to avoid emotion in our relations with God, or at least we prefer to depersonalize prayer.

A New Pentecost?, p. 97.

Your prayer should always be an intimate conversation with a loving Father. Put in a few requests, but
don't center your prayer on a "getting" theme.
Remember what Jesus said:

> Your Father knows what you need before you
> ask him.

Matthew 6:8

If you're serious about enjoying a personal relationship with the Father, you need to be serious about
talking and listening to him. Scripture says our model
for a personal relationship, Jesus, spent whole nights
in prayer. And when he prayed, the conversation was
to a Father who was very near and personal.

It's through this personal prayer that guidance
comes. Jesus preceded every major event in his life by
spending time alone with the Father. For example,
Scripture tells us that once Jesus spent a whole night
in prayer and then at daybreak called the twelve
disciples apart to make them apostles *(Luke 6:12-16).*
Jesus recognized this prayer-induced guidance when,
at the Last Supper, he prayed "for these *you* have
given me . . ." *(John 17:9).* Yes, Jesus used prayer for
guidance.

So guidance will often come directly through
prayer. It comes through meditations, through Scriptures read during prayer and through an intuitive
knowledge — a silent voice within our spirits saying,
"My son (daughter), this is what I wish of you. . . ."
Let me repeat, an attitude of expectant faith is absolutely necessary. Expect the Father to speak in

prayer. After all, what loving Father would refuse to speak to his son or daughter?

COMMUNITY

True Christian community can be a powerful balancing factor in guidance. A community of people who live in a personal relationship with the Father and who believe that he will guide them through his Spirit, will provide a valuable means of very objective guidance. You see, I might be swayed by my own personal inclinations, but a group of committed Christians most likely will not. The problem, of course, is that such communities are hard to find. Steve Clark writes:

> A Christian must have an environment in his life in which Christianity is openly accepted, talked about, and lived if he is going to be able to live a very vital Christian life. If he does not have this, his whole life as a Christian will be weak and might even die away. Yet fewer and fewer Catholics are finding such an environment.
>
> *Building Christian Community*, p. 33.

When I talk about "Christian community," I'm referring to a group of people (the size is unimportant) who are willing to be more than friends. They're willing to give of themselves to support each other, and to be committed to one another. When you can trust yourself to such a Christian group, you obtain a powerful source of growth and guidance. These people, like you, must have the same kind of expectant faith in a Father who guides and instructs.

Today, in general, only the Cursillo and Charismatic Renewal movements are producing such groups and they, unfortunately, are not active in every parish. Nevertheless, if such a group is available, join and become committed to it. It may turn out to be your most powerful source of guidance.

WITNESS OF THE HOLY SPIRIT

St. John the Apostle wrote:

> But as for you, Christ has poured out his Spirit on you. As long as his Spirit remains in you, you do not need anyone to teach you. For his Spirit teaches you about everything, and what he teaches is true, not false. Obey the Spirit's teaching, then, and remain in Christ.
>
> *1 John 2:27 (TEV)*

One of the main reasons you've received the Spirit is for teaching and guidance. And if you're really being guided by the Holy Spirit, he'll leave his mark on you. Yes, the fruit of the Spirit will gradually become evident in your life. Again, St. Paul recalls that . . .

> . . . the fruit of the Spirit is love, joy, peace, patient endurance, kindness, generosity, faith, mildness, and chastity.
>
> *Galatians 5:22*

So these qualities are a ''spiritual barometer'' to the committed Christian. If they're evident and seem to be slowly growing, you can be sure you're generally following the Father's direction; if not, something is wrong.

But of all these fruits, I believe peace is the easiest to apply to guidance. St. Paul said that "Christ's peace must reign in your hearts" *(Colossians 3:15)*. So if that peace isn't there, you should ask yourself whether or not you've heard the message correctly. Of course this isn't an infallible sign. A lack of peace could be caused by other things. But, in general, if you start along a certain path believing that you're following the Father's Will, and find that peace escapes you, then stop and take another look at your original discernment. If your lack of peace is caused by some other spiritual or physical problem, then go ahead on that path. If not, your lack of peace means that you've ventured outside the Father's Will. You may find this test of inner peace a bit awkward at first, but with practice it becomes quite natural.

LEARNING TO BE GUIDED

So now we have eight sources for guidance. What's next? Well, as I said before, guidance isn't automatic; you can't just switch it on or off. As important as it is to the Christian life, only sincere Christians can learn it. Yes, it does have to be learned. Not only in the sense of learning what the sources are, but in the sense of learning how to properly use those sources. Of course this idea of learning guidance isn't new. Look at the Psalms and you'll see:

> Your ways, O Lord, make known to me; *teach me* your paths, Guide me in your truth and *teach me,* for you are God my savior.
>
> *Psalm 25:4-5*

Show me, O Lord, your way, and lead me on a
level path.

Psalm 27:11

Teach me to do your will, for you are my God.
Psalm 143:10

Now the most important thing you must learn is
that the eight categories work together in guidance,
one complementing the other. For instance, you might
feel the Father's guidance as you combine prayer and
scripture reading. To confirm that guidance, try talking it over with a spiritually mature friend or perhaps a
priest (i.e. Christian community). Use circumstances
or the inner witness of the Spirit's peace to add to your
confidence. Use as many independent sources as you
can but as a rule, use no less than three.

Now some people get discouraged and quit trying
before they ever really get started. Remember,
guidance is learned over a period of time. Even if
you've memorized all the sources and understand how
they work together, you still must learn to trust the
Father. And that process is a long one for most people.
It might be compared to the trust which develops in a
good Christian marriage. It's developed through
shared experiences; in other words, you must experience the Father's hand guiding you repeatedly
before you truly trust him. Only when trust matures,
can guidance mature.

PROBLEMS IN GUIDANCE

This wonderful experience, guidance, does give
newcomers some problems. Most of these, however,
will be overcome as you gain experience. And

remember, the more you seek independent sources to check guidance, the fewer problems you will have.

One problem area people venture into when first experiencing guidance is ''illuminism.'' It's characterized by an attitude which says, ''The Father is guiding me in *everything* I do and I know his Will at all times.'' This simply isn't true because by doing so, the Father would be turning you into a robot, and that would be violating your free will. The Father created you with intelligence and common sense; he expects you to use these tools to handle everyday decisions. Be careful, I've seen people slip into this area of illuminism simply to avoid ordinary decisions. That's not what the Father had in mind when he said he desired to guide you.

When Jesus introduced himself as the ''Good Shepherd'' he was picking up a theme that the Father had given Jewish prophets centuries before. Psalm 23 is a good example of this image. The Good Shepherd is portrayed as a man who guides, protects and loves his sheep, even to the point of giving his life. Now it's important to understand that the Father didn't introduce this concept with only one point in mind. The image of shepherd and sheep, in fact, carries many truths about our relationship with the Father. In guidance, for example, it can help eliminate the problem of illuminism. You see, the shepherd does *guide* the sheep to pasture, but he doesn't tell them how to walk, when to eat, or which tuft of grass to chew. The sheep have enough common sense to do that for themselves. And you, hopefully, have even more common sense than sheep. So minor details like tufts of grass are left to the discernment of the Father's sheep.

Now when I say that the Father wants you to make common, everyday decisions using your own intelligence, I am not saying that the details of your life are unimportant to him. These details are in fact very important, and he is concerned with every aspect of your life. However, he doesn't want you to simply sit back in your easy chair and have him make all the decisions. Well then, what exactly does the Father want? Simply this: he asks you to *walk in faith.* Remember our discussion of "expectant faith?" It's a faith that trusts and expects things to happen. So the Father asks you to have an attitude that he indeed is with you and will guide you very specifically when need be. And you, for your part, need to believe in the Father's guidance and learn to trust him. The noted Christian author, Don Basham, explains:

> Most Christians don't want to walk by faith, they want to walk by *certainty.* But God has ordained that we walk by *faith,* not by certainty. When people say to me, "But I'm not sure what God wants me to do," I reply, "Friend, if you could be sure, it wouldn't take any faith. God will not let you be 100 percent sure."
>
> *How God Guides Us,* p. 11.

Mr. Basham goes on to speak of guidance as a ship's rudder. Now the rudder is useless if the ship isn't moving. So the Father asks you to keep moving through daily decisions and, at the same time, seeking guidance through valid sources. Trust him to move the rudder of your life as you use your common sense and intelligence to make obvious decisions. Sometimes you'll know for sure that you're on the right track, often you won't. But it really doesn't matter. Walking by faith means you're trusting him even when you can't "feel" his guidance.

201

Of course I'm not saying that you shouldn't want to seek assurance of the Father's guidance. You should. But when it doesn't come, don't panic. Simply keep moving, keep seeking and especially, keep trusting. You can be sure he's moving the rudder.

Now sometimes you'll be doing all these things as you suppose you should, and find that things aren't working out. Your guidance will sometimes come in the form of closed doors or blocked paths. That's when faith is really tested. That's when you're asked to say, "Okay Father, I trust in you. I'll take that other path even if it's less appealing." You see, often your desire for something blocks out the Father's guidance. Your desire, so to speak, overwhelms the Father's input. Then he has only one choice left — he must close the door or block the path — and you must trust.

Another problem area is called "fundamentalism." It leads a person to interpret the Bible or other sources of guidance quite literally; therefore it can be a source of serious *mis*interpretation. Scripture in particular must be carefully interpreted and throughout the centuries our Church has been quick to point that out. Of course there have been some people who, in trying to avoid fundamentalism, have made a far more serious mistake by saying that nothing in Scripture should be taken literally. That is not true. There are a great many things in Scripture, and in Jesus' Gospels in particular, that the Father wants us to take quite literally. Not only literally but, I might add, *seriously*. Perhaps the cure for avoiding fundamentalism is far worse than the problem itself.

A good knowledge of basic scriptural principles, a Bible commentary and the guidance of a mature Christian friend or priest will usually steer you clear of fundamentalism. Also follow that general rule of always seeking other independent sources to confirm guidance.

In his earthly ministry, Jesus was constantly running into yet another guidance problem. You could best call it "sign seeking."

> With a sigh from the depths of his spirit he (Jesus) said, "Why does this age seek a sign? I assure you, no such sign will be given it!"
>
> *Mark 8:12*

You see, Jesus was frustrated by "religious" people who always needed a sign before they would believe anything. This same attitude can enter people who are seeking guidance and it usually stems from an unwillingness to *trust*. The "scriptural roulette" I talked about earlier can easily turn into sign seeking. However, all guidance sources are open to this problem. The Father will tolerate sign seeking as you begin your spiritual walk, and he'll truly give you some clear signs of love and guidance. But as you grow in spiritual maturity, he expects you to become less dependent on signs and more trusting of him. That doesn't mean the Holy Spirit will never lead you to seek signs after you're a fairly mature Christian, but it does mean that you shouldn't need as many as when you were learning guidance. In other words, excessive sign seeking points to a lack of trust and a lack of maturity.

The Father isn't out to make puppets of us through guidance, but rather to create *mature* men and women who seek his Will and follow wherever he leads. Sons and daughters who, like Jesus, constantly search for his Will in all significant matters, yet are mature enough to avoid traps like illuminism, indecision and fundamentalism. People of depth and character who understand guidance not as a blueprint for life, but as a voyage through life with their Fathers at the helm. Yes, it's an adventure — a rich and exciting experience that will show you, better than anything else, just how loving and caring the Father is. Don't pass guidance by or push it aside for a later time. Every sincere Christian needs it.

FIXING YOUR MIND
ON THE RELATIONSHIP

The prophet Jeremiah recognized the Lord's guidance when he said:

> You know, O Lord, that man is not master of his way; Man's course is not within his choice, nor is it for him to direct his step.
>
> *Jeremiah 10:23*

Yet even the great Jeremiah didn't dream that Jesus would come to proclaim that not only guidance, but "sonship" was offered to men. He wouldn't dare think that "Abba" would be our prayer. Still John writes:

> See what love the Father has bestowed on us in letting us be called children of God! *Yet that is what we are.*
>
> *1 John 3:1*

Guidance and every other aspect of your Christian life must revolve around this one, incredible, divinely revealed truth: *You are a son (daughter) of the Father.* If you want growth in this relationship with your Father, I'll let you in on the secret of success. Simply *know* that that is true. You may be weak in prayer, knowledge of Scripture or the techniques of guidance, but that truth will make you so strong that any weak areas will eventually be overcome. I've developed a method that can help you do this. It isn't a tricky technique or some new spiritual exercise. It's simply "the truth" coming alive in you. What you must do, and do with determination, is fix your mind on that one essential truth: "You *are* a son or daughter of the Father." When I say "fix" your mind on this truth, I mean it must be foremost in your mind, the center of your attention, and influence everything you do or say or think.

I've found that by adopting three simple rules in my life, I'm able to very effectively fix my mind on that truth. Try them yourself.

1. I wake each morning to the question: "Who am I?" The answer I give myself is always the same: "I'm son, servant and beloved of my Father." I'll face things in the day ahead that will try to deceive me and deny that awesome truth, but now as I wake it's foremost in my mind.

2. In every new situation I enter during the day, I myself again ask: "Who am I?" The same answer persists: "I am son, servant and beloved of my Father." This isn't easy, but it's important. It keeps my mind in tune with what Father Brennan Manning has called "The order of the really real." All that is in the world will be passing away. Only my relationship with the Father has any lasting value. That relationship is the "really real" thing in every circumstance of every minute of every

day.

3. I've made it a rule to change my prayer habits, not the length or place of prayer, but the "words" of prayer. I previously used "God" or "Lord" when talking with the Father. Now I use *Father* or *Abba* only. I can't give you any good reasons why this is important, but it does seem to be very important. If you'll search the Gospels, you'll find that Jesus always begins prayer with "Father" or "Abba." Now aren't we supposed to imitate him? Remember St. Paul's words:

> The *proof* that you are sons is the fact that God has sent forth into our hearts the spirit of his Son which cries out "Abba!" ("Father!").
>
> *Galatians* 4:6

Follow these three simple rules and you'll find that each day will bring you closer and closer to this eternal, joyous truth: "You *are* son (daughter), servant and beloved of the Father." Amen. Come, Lord Jesus.

BIBLIOGRAPHY

Recommended Readings

Personal Relationship

1. Lange, Joseph, and Anthony Cushing. *Friendship With Jesus.* Paulist Press, New York, N.Y./Paramus, N.J., 1974, 208 pp.
   An excellent and very practical guide to knowing Jesus through a personal relationship.
2. Manning, Brennan, T.O.R. *The Gentle Revolutionaries.* Dimension Books, Denville, N.J., 1976, 140 pp.
   This book offers valuable insights into exactly what it means to be a Christian and to live in a personal relationship with the Father.

Openness to the Holy Spirit

3. Kosicki, George, C.S.B., Editor. *The Lord is My Shepherd — Witness of Priests.* Servant Books, Ann Arbor, Mich., 1973, 129 pp.
4. Manney, James and Louise Bourassa, Editors. *Come and See.* Servant Books, Ann Arbor, Mich., 1976, 170 pp.
5. Manning, Brennan, T.O.R. *Prophets and Lovers*

— *In Search of the Holy Spirit.* Dimension Books, Denville, N.J., 1976, 125 pp.

Prayer

6. Martin, Ralph. *Hungry For God: Practical Help in Personal Prayer.* Doubleday & Co., Inc., Garden City, N.Y., 1974, 168 pp.

Scripture

7. Martin, George. *Reading Scripture as the Word of God: Practical Approaches and Attitudes.* Servant Books, Ann Arbor, Mich., 1975. 188 pp.

General

8. Lewis, C.S. *Mere Christianity.* The Macmillan Co., New York, N.Y. 1952, 190 pp.
9. Suenens, Cardinal Leon Joseph. *A New Pentecost?* The Seabury Press, New York, N.Y., 1975, 239 pp.

Other Books Referenced Herein

1. Abbott and Gallagher, (Editors). *The Documents of Vatican II.* The American Press, New York, N.Y., 1966, 794 pp.
2. National Conference of Catholic Bishops. *Basic Teachings For Catholic Religious Education.* United States Catholic Conference, Washington, D.C., 1973, 36 pp.

3. Field, Anne, O.S.B. *The Binding of the Strong Man — the Teachings of St. Leo the Great.* Servant Books, Ann Arbor, Mich., 1976, 113 pp.

4. Wilhelm, Anthony. *Christ Among Us.* 2nd Ed., Paulist Press, New York, N.Y., 1975, 440 pp.

5. Clark, Stephen B. *Building Christian Communities.* Ave Maria Press, Notre Dame, Ind., 1972, 189 pp.

6. Basham, Don. *How God Guides Us.* Manna Christian Outreach, Greensburg, Pa., 1975.

7. Marty, Martin E. *A Short History of Christianity.* William Collins & World Publishing Co., New York, N.Y., 1975, 384 pp.

Additional books from
LIVING FLAME PRESS
Available at your bookstore or from
Living Flame Press, Locust Valley, N.Y. 11560

TO COMFORT AND CONFRONT
Biblical Reflections   **2.95**

Kenneth Overberg, S.J. We are challenged today through the timelessness of Scripture to meet the needs of our evolving world and take action. Individuals will find fresh insight and questions for private prayer. Communities and prayer groups will find stimulating starting points for shared prayer.

WHOLENESS
The Legacy of Jesus   **2.50**

Adolfo Quezada presents practical and spiritual perspectives to those seeking purpose and meaning in their lives. He faces the reality that we are all broken by the impact of suffering and torn by the pull of distractions. He offers hope and direction toward a more abundant life.

PRESENCE THROUGH THE WORD   **2.50**

Sr. Evelyn Ann Schumacher, O.S.F. Personal intimacy with the Father, the Son and the Holy Spirit is meant for every Christian. Experience of that presence is attainable in our lives as we trace the ancient quest of others through the pages of Scripture.

SPIRITUAL DIRECTION
Contemporary Readings   5.95

Edited by Kevin Culligan, O.C.D. The revitalized ministry
of spiritual direction is one of the surest signs of renewal in today's Church. In this book seventeen leading
writers and spiritual directors discuss history, meaning,
demands and practice of this ministry. Readers of the
book should include not just a spiritual elite, but the en-
tire Church — men and women, clergy and laity, members of religious communities.

PRAYER:
The Eastern Tradition   2.95

Andrew Ryder, S.C.J. In the East there is no sharp
distinction between prayer and theology. Far from being
divorced they are seen as supporting and completing
each other. One is impossible without the other.
Theology is not an end in itself, but rather a means, a
way to union with God.

THE RETURNING SUN
Hope for a Broken World   2.50

George A. Maloney, S.J. In this collection of meditations, the author draws on his own experiences rooted
in Eastern Christianity to aid the reader to enter into the
world of the "heart." It is hoped that through contemplation of this material he/she will discover the return of
the inextinguishable Sun of the universe, Jesus Christ,
in a new and more experiential way.

LIVING HERE AND HEREAFTER
Christian Dying,
Death and Resurrection   **2.95**

Msgr. David E. Rosage. The author offers great comfort to us by dispelling our fears and anxieties about our life after this earthly sojourn. Based on God's Word as presented in Sacred Scripture, these brief daily meditations help us understand more clearly and deeply the meaning of suffering and death.

PRAYING WITH SCRIPTURE
IN THE HOLY LAND
Daily Meditations With the Risen Jesus   **3.50**

Msgr. David E. Rosage. Herein is offered a daily meeting with the Risen Jesus in those Holy Places which He sanctified by His human presence. Three hundred and sixty-five scripture texts are selected and blended with the pilgrimage experiences of the author, a retreat master, and well-known writer on prayer.

DISCERNMENT:
Seeking God in Every Situation   **3.50**

Rev. Chris Aridas. "Many Christians struggle with ways to seek, know and understand God's plan for their lives. This book is prayerful, refreshing and very practical for daily application. It is one to be read and used regularly, not just read" *(Ray Roh, O.S.B.).*

A DESERT PLACE   **2.50**

Adolfo Quezada. "The author speaks of the desert place deep within, where one can share the joy of the Lord's presence, but also the pain of the nights of our own faithlessness" *(Pecos Benedictine).*

MOURNING: THE HEALING JOURNEY   2.95

Rev. Kenneth J. Zanca. Comfort for those who have lost a loved one. Out of the grief suffered in the loss of both parents within two months, this young priest has written a sensitive, sympathetic yet humanly constructive book to help others who have lost loved ones. This is a book that might be given to the newly bereaved.

THE BORN-AGAIN CATHOLIC   3.95

Albert H. Boudreau. This book presents an authoritative imprimatur treatment of today's most interesting religious issue. The author, a Catholic layman, looks at Church tradition past and present and shows that the born-again experience is not only valid, but actually is Catholic Christianity at its best. The exciting experience is not only investigated, but the reader is guided into revitalizing his or her own Christian experience. The informal style, colorful personal experiences, and helpful diagrams make this book enjoyable and profitable reading.

WISDOM INSTRUCTS HER CHILDREN
The Power of the Spirit and the Word   3.50

John Randall, S.T.D. The author believes that now is God's time for "wisdom." Through the Holy Spirit, "power" has become much more accessible in the Church. Wisdom, however, lags behind and the result is imbalance and disarray. The Spirit is now seeking to pour forth a wisdom we never dreamed possible. This outpouring could lead us into a new age of Jesus Christ! This is a badly needed, most important book, not only for the Charismatic Renewal, but for the whole Church.

DISCOVERING
PATHWAYS TO PRAYER   2.95

Msgr. David E. Rosage. Following Jesus was never meant to be dull, or worse, just duty-filled. Those who would aspire to a life of prayer and those who have already begun, will find this book amazingly thorough in its scripture-punctuated approach.

"A simple but profound book which explains the many ways and forms of prayer by which the person hungering for closer union with God may find him" *(Emmanuel Spillane, O.C.S.O., Abbot, Our Lady of the Holy Trinity Abbey, Huntsville, Utah).*

GRAINS OF WHEAT   2.95

Kelly B. Kelly. This little book of words received in prayer is filled with simple yet often profound leadings, exhortations and encouragement for daily living. Within the pages are insights to help one function as a Christian, day by day, minute by minute.

BREAD FOR THE EATING   2.95

Kelly B. Kelly. Sequel to the popular *Grains of Wheat*, this small book of words received in prayer draws the reader closer to God through the imagery of wheat being processed into bread. The author shares her love of the natural world.

DESERT SILENCE:
A Way of Prayer for an Unquiet Age   2.50

Alan J. Placa and *Brendan Riordan.* The pioneering efforts of the men and women of the early church who went out into the desert to find union with the Lord has relevance for those of us today who are seeking the pure uncluttered desert place within to have it filled with the loving silence of God's presence.

WHO IS THIS GOD YOU PRAY TO?   2.95

Bernard Hayes, C.R. Who is God for me? How do I "picture" him? This book helps us examine our negative images of God and, through prayer, be led to those images which Jesus reveals to us and which can help us grow into a deeper and more valid relationship with God as Father, Lover, Redeemer, etc.

UNION WITH THE LORD IN PRAYER
Beyond Meditation to Affective
Prayer Aspiration and Contemplation   1.50

Venard Polusney, O.Carm. "A magnificent piece of work. It touches on all the essential points of contemplative prayer. Yet it brings such a sublime subject down to the level of comprehension of the 'man in the street,' and in such an encouraging way" *(Abbot James Fox, O.C.S.O., former superior of Thomas Merton at the Abbey of Gethsemane).*

ATTAINING SPIRITUAL MATURITY
FOR CONTEMPLATION
(According to St. John of the Cross)   1.50

Venard Polusney, O. Carm. "I heartily recommend this work with great joy that at last the sublime teachings of St. John of the Cross have been brought down to the understanding of the ordinary Christian without at the same time watering them down. For all (particularly for charismatic Christians) hungry for greater contemplation" *(George A. Maloney, S.J., editor of Diakonia, Professor of Patristics and Spirituality, Fordham University).*

PRAYING WITH MARY   2.95

Msgr. David E. Rosage. This book is one avenue which will help us discover ways and means to satisfy our longing for prayer and a more personal knowledge of God. Prayer was Mary's life-style. As we come to know more about her life of prayer we will find ourselves imitating her in our approach to God.

LINGER WITH ME
Moments Aside With Jesus   3.50

Rev. Msgr. David E. Rosage. God is calling us to a listening posture in prayer in the desire to experience him at the very core of our being. Monsignor Rosage helps us to "come by ourselves apart" daily and listen to what Jesus is telling us in scripture.

THE BOOK OF REVELATION:
What Does It Really Say?   2.50

John Randall, S.T.D. The most discussed book of the Bible today is examined by a scripture expert in relation to much that has been published on the truth. A simply written and revealing presentation. The basis for many discussion groups.

LIVING FLAME PRESS
Box 74, Locust Valley, N.Y. 11560

QUANTITY

_____	Wholeness: The Legacy of Jesus — 2.50
_____	Presence Through the Word — 2.50
_____	To Comfort and Confront — 2.95
_____	Spiritual Direction — 5.95
_____	The Returning Sun — 2.50
_____	Prayer: the Eastern Tradition — 2.95
_____	Living Here and Hereafter — 2.95
_____	Praying With Scripture in the Holy Land — 3.50
_____	Discernment — 3.50
_____	A Desert Place — 2.50
_____	Mourning: The Healing Journey — 2.95
_____	The Born-Again Catholic — 3.95
_____	Wisdom Instructs Her Children — 3.50
_____	Discovering Pathways to Prayer — 2.95
_____	Grains of Wheat — 2.95
_____	Bread for the Eating — 2.95
_____	Desert Silence — 2.50
_____	Who Is This God You Pray To? — 2.95
_____	Union With the Lord in Prayer — 1.50
_____	Attaining Spiritual Maturity — 1.50
_____	Praying With Mary — 2.95
_____	Linger With Me — 3.50
_____	Book of Revelation — 2.50
_____	Seeking Purity of Heart — 2.50
_____	To Live as Jesus Did — 2.95

NAME _____

ADDRESS _____

CITY _____ STATE _____ ZIP_____

Payment enclosed. Kindly include $.70 postage and handling on orders up to $5; $1.00 on orders up to $10; more than $10 but less than $50 add 10% of total; over $50 add 8% of total. Canadian residents add 20% exchange rate, plus postage and handling.

LIVING FLAME PRESS
Box 74, Locust Valley, N.Y. 11560

QUANTITY

_____	Wholeness: The Legacy of Jesus — 2.50
_____	Presence Through the Word — 2.50
_____	To Comfort and Confront — 2.95
_____	Spiritual Direction — 5.95
_____	The Returning Sun — 2.50
_____	Prayer: the Eastern Tradition — 2.95
_____	Living Here and Hereafter — 2.95
_____	Praying With Scripture in the Holy Land — 3.50
_____	Discernment — 3.50
_____	A Desert Place — 2.50
_____	Mourning: The Healing Journey — 2.95
_____	The Born-Again Catholic — 3.95
_____	Wisdom Instructs Her Children — 3.50
_____	Discovering Pathways to Prayer — 2.95
_____	Grains of Wheat — 2.95
_____	Bread for the Eating — 2.95
_____	Desert Silence — 2.50
_____	Who Is This God You Pray To? — 2.95
_____	Union With the Lord in Prayer — 1.50
_____	Attaining Spiritual Maturity — 1.50
_____	Praying With Mary — 2.95
_____	Linger With Me — 3.50
_____	Book of Revelation — 2.50
_____	Seeking Purity of Heart — 2.50
_____	To Live as Jesus Did — 2.95

NAME _____

ADDRESS _____

CITY _____ STATE _____ ZIP_____

Payment enclosed. Kindly include $.70 postage and handling on orders up to $5; $1.00 on orders up to $10; more than $10 but less than $50 add 10% of total; over $50 add 8% of total. Canadian residents add 20% exchange rate, plus postage and handling.